IIS 6 Programm

MW00981741

Christopher Ambler
Alex Homer
Michael De Marco
Srinivasa Sivakumar
S Vaidyaraman

® Wrox Press Ltd.

IIS 6 Programming Handbook

First published March 2003

Published by Wrox Press Ltd,
Arden House, 1102 Warwick Road, Acocks Green,
Birmingham, B27 6BH
United Kingdom
Printed in the United States
ISBN 1-86100-839-2

Trademark Acknowledgments

Credits

Authors
Christopher Ambler
Alex Homer
Michael De Marco
Srinivasa Sivakumar
S Vaidyaraman

Technical Reviewers
Natalia Bortniker
Mark Horner
Erick Sgarbi
Jon Shute
Morgan Skinner
Chandu Thota
Sakhr Youness

Technical Editors
Nilesh Parmar
Nikhil Salvi

Commissioning Editor
Douglas Paterson

Managing Editors
Emma Batch
Kalpana Garde

Project Managers
Safiulla Shakir
Charlotte Smith

Production Coordinator
Sarah Hall

Indexer
Michael Brinkman

Proof Reader
Susan Nettleton

Cover
Natalie O'Donnell

About the Authors

Christopher Ambler

Christopher's first memory of computers dates back to 1976 when he was 9 years old, and sat down at a "Dataspeed 40" terminal at the Pacific Telephone frame where his Uncle worked. After that, if it had to do with computers, he was interested.

Christopher has been a developer, web designer, analyst, and consultant, with over 18 years of experience. He has worked at Microsoft as a developer on Exchange Server and Passport, and as a technical writer in the marketing group as well as on the new IIS 6.0 SDK.

Currently, he is an independent consultant for companies looking to make the move to .NET technologies, and lives near Redmond, Washington with his wife and two children, where he codes for fun, produces electronic music, plays poker, and attempts to perfect his photography technique.

First and foremost, I would like to thank Eric Stenson, development lead on HTTP.sys, at Microsoft. I would also like to recognize those with whom I've worked on the IIS 6.0 SDK for their valuable assistance, including Janet Fisher, Sharon Slade, Eric Deily, and Wade Hilmo at Microsoft.

I'd like to thank my wife Lisa, and children Caitlin and Jason, for putting up with Daddy disappearing into his office. And to my parents, for understanding that computers were more than just a hobby. Finally, I would like to thank everyone at Wrox Press, especially Douglas Patterson, Daniel Kent, and Charlotte Smith, for making my first experience with them a good one.

Alex Homer

Alex Homer lives and works in the idyllic rural surroundings of the Derbyshire Dales in England. With the help of three (usually sleeping) cats and a very understanding wife, he spends his time playing with all the latest technologies, the newest hardware and the flakiest beta code he can find. As he says, "Someone's got to do it!" However, as a safety precaution, he always makes sure that all the servers have a large white cross-painted on the side to locate the point where percussive maintenance is applied.

Other than an inability to get a decent computer insurance quotation, he leads a quiet, peaceful and undisturbed existence away from the hustle and bustle of everyday life. In fact, after a lifetime spent working in almost every industry (other than computing), he can't believe that he actually gets paid for doing this.

Michael De Marco

Michael Alexander De Marco has been a software consultant for over 23 years. In his role as a consultant he utilizes C/C++, Java, C#, VB and MFC. He loves technologies using COM/DCOM/MTS/ASP/JSP. His focus is object-oriented programming with Microsoft DNA & J2EE. He teaches programming & technology courses at Learning Tree University. He can be reached at michael_de_marco@hotmail.com

Srinivasa Sivakumar

Srinivasa Sivakumar is a Sr. Architect, developer and writer. He specializes in web and mobile technologies using Microsoft solutions. He has co-authored many Wrox books and has also written technical articles for ASP Today, and C# Today. In his free time he likes to watch Tamil movies and listens to Tamil sound tracks (especially one's sung by Mr. S.P Balasubramaniyam).

This is my 10th book project with Wrox and this is a happiest moment. I'm really grateful to Wrox Press to making this happen and my special thanks goes to Charlotte, Doug, Dan, Matt, Cil, Emma, Beckie, Nick, Andrew, and Laura for their help with my books. I'd like to extend my special thanks to Richard Ersek, Janet Fisher, Adam Overton, Raymond Ho, Bruno K. Da Costa, and Alvin Loh of Microsoft IIS6 team for their timely support.

S Vaidyaraman

Vaidyaraman has been specializing in IT since 1998 and is currently associated with HCL Infosystems, Chennai. His area of expertise has been in Microsoft Technologies and he publishes articles/papers for various web sites, which include Wrox sites like ASP Today and C# Today. He is deeply fascinated by .NET related technologies and keeps exploring the bright new features they offer. In his spare time he could be found surfing the web, playing chess and watching cricket.

I would like to thank my parents for their support and encouragement over the years without which nothing would have been possible. I would also like to thank the Wrox team including the project managers, reviewers and technical editors for their excellent support throughout the project.

IIS 6

Programming

Handbook

Table of
Contents

Table of Contents

IIS 6

Programming

Handbook

Introduction

Introduction

In today's internet world, web servers occupy the most important position, the one between the users and the web applications. They are essentially the gatekeepers of the ever-changing internet world, and are responsible for providing an environment for both the client and the servers to work in. This puts tremendous responsibility on web administrators, who have to ensure that the server is exploited to the maximum to fulfill the policies of the organization or enterprise that the server belongs to.

IIS 6.0 is Microsoft's latest web server offering, and incorporates features that ensure that your server is ready for the future of Internet. It offers reliable, scalable, secure, and manageable web server capabilities that could be used by both programmers and administrators to develop and implement the latest in web technologies.

Expectedly, IIS 6.0 improves upon its previous versions in all aspects, while at the same time providing a number of new features that signal a drastic change in the design of the new server. The most significant is in the realm of security, where IIS 6.0 provides the administrator with a host of options to enforce an aggressive security policy. The request architecture of IIS has been completely redone. In fact, many new features and enhancements of IIS 6.0 find their root in the new request architecture. The separation of user and kernel mode code alone entails improved reliability, performance, and inherent security. The Worker Processes, Application Pools, Isolation modes, and Web Gardens promise enhanced performance and scalability.

This book serves as a detailed guide into the workings of IIS 6.0 architecture as well as a handy reference for programmers who want to develop web applications and deploy them on this server.

What Do You Need?

To make use of this book, you need to have access to an installation of Windows Server 2003.

Book Outline

Below is a detailed outline of what this book covers chapter by chapter:

Chapter 1 – An Overview of IIS 6.0

The first chapter is a brief overview of what the reader can expect from IIS 6.0 and from the rest of the book. It lists the significant features of IIS 6.0, and more specifically in the areas of security, reliability, performance, scalability, administration, and development. It familiarizes the reader with new features of IIS 6.0 as well as providing comparisons with its predecessors along the way. In addition to short introductions to the specific features, the chapter also provides references to the individual chapters where more detailed information can be found.

Chapter 2 – The New Request Architecture

This chapter explores the new request architecture, which is the highlight of IIS 6.0. It introduces and discusses the kernel mode, HTTP.sys, and the Web Administration Service (WAS). The chapter introduces the new Worker Process Isolation Mode and the backward compatible IIS 5 Isolation mode. The readers will be familiarized with the new concepts of Worker Processes and Application pools, and how to configure IIS 6.0 to take advantage of the new features such as Web Gardens and processor affinity to improve scalability and performance.

Chapter 3 – Security in IIS 6.0

This chapter discusses security in IIS 6.0. Security in IIS 6.0 is more than just disabling and enabling features and capabilities, and covers a number of different realms. IIS 6.0 allows you to control the security picture at different levels, from a whole-server standpoint all the way down to individual files. In this chapter, we will look at how to secure your server, by considering the extension management, web site and FTP site authentication, access control, cryptography, application pool/worker process identities, and timeouts and limits

Chapter 4 – The XML Metabase

In this chapter, we will look at the way that this new configuration system works, the structure of the data, and how we can manipulate it in different ways. We discuss what the configuration data format looks like, and how this simplifies administration, how security is implemented and managed on the configuration information, and how we can edit this data while IIS is running.

Chapter 5 – Administering IIS 6.0

In this chapter we discuss how to administer IIS 6.0, in enough detail for the programmer to feel confident with the environment. We discuss command-line administration, programmatic administration, remote administration, and configuring Quality of Service. We also discuss how to take backups, and import or export configurations and settings of IIS 6.0.

Chapter 6 – Logging

This chapter discusses the different types of logging and how to decide between them. We explore how to configure each type, and how to make use of the logs generated by the traffic to your site. We discuss W3C Extended, NCSA, IIS, ODBC, Custom, and Centralized Binary logging.

Chapter 7 – ISAPI

This chapter talks about the ISAPI extensions and filters. It begins by discussing the ISAPI models in the previous versions of IIS. We discuss, in detail, the new extensions features in ISAPI, ISAPI security, developing ISAPI extensions and filters, and debugging ISAPI extensions and filters.

Chapter 8 – COM and COM+ services

In this chapter, we look at how IIS 6.0 differs from previous versions, in terms of support for COM and COM+ services. We explore the new services and components that are available for programmers. We also cover how the NET Framework integrates with IIS 6.0.

IIS 6

Programming

Handbook

1

An Overview of IIS 6.0

As the Internet matures, so do the requirements for the servers that run the Internet's critical components. Internet Information Services (IIS) 6.0 incorporates a number of new features, some evolutionary and some revolutionary, as well as many enhancements to existing features that clearly demonstrate that it is keeping pace with the changing Internet. IIS 6.0 represents a significant improvement over previous versions, incorporating enhancements required by the rapidly changing Internet environment.

IIS 6.0 includes the enhancements in the following areas of the web application server platform:

- ❏ Security
- ❏ Reliability
- ❏ Performance and Scalability
- ❏ Administration
- ❏ Development

The Road to IIS 6.0

Before jumping into the "what's new" in IIS 6.0, let's take a look at what issues in previous versions of IIS have driven the enhancements found in IIS 6.0.

What Stands Out - The Highlights

There are a number of new features in IIS 6.0 designed to enhance functionality, performance, and reliability over previous versions. The most significant highlight in terms of the evolution of IIS has to be the new kernel-mode listener, `HTTP.sys`. Whereas previous versions of IIS utilized their own `Winsock/afd.sys` communication drivers, `HTTP.sys` is an integral part of the Windows.NET networking subsystem. Previous versions of IIS relied on their own Winsock listener, running with high privileges. Web applications like ISAPI extensions could be loaded into this process, creating both a security threat as well as a reliability problem – if the ISAPI were to crash, it would take the listener down with it. `HTTP.sys` addresses these problems by running in kernel mode and being completely isolated from web application code. Not only does that provide significant performance gains, but it also prevents any user code from affecting the operation of the listener.

IIS 6.0 is, in essence, a "locked-down" server when first installed, providing a default configuration with as small a security risk as possible. Individual application extensions must be specifically enabled, as compared to previous versions that had all functionality enabled by default. In previous versions of IIS, the ability to run web applications out-of-process meant accepting a performance hit in exchange for more isolation. IIS 6.0 introduces Worker Process Isolation Mode, which combines the benefits of process isolation without the performance degradation associated with multiple process boundary transitions. Worker Process Isolation Mode, in concert with `HTTP.sys` addresses both the performance and reliability concerns of previous versions of IIS.

Configuration information has, until now, been stored in a binary metabase. IIS 6.0 moves that configuration metabase into a text file and formats it as XML, allowing for editing with any text editor. Furthermore, the metabase can now be edited while IIS is running, without the need for restarting the server.

ISAPI has been given a number of new features to address issues that were encountered in IIS 5. Most notably, there are a large number of developers who need to be able to process request entity data before it gets handled. In IIS 5 and earlier, although this functionality was supposed to be offered through the `READ_RAW_DATA` filter facility; the truth is that this cannot be reliably done (for reasons that are well beyond the scope of this chapter).

IIS 6.0 specifically addresses this issue by creating wildcard scriptmaps and the `HSE_REQ_EXEC_URL` server support function. ExecuteURL has been noted as the standout ISAPI feature for IIS 6.0, allowing developers to incorporate "filter-like" tasks in an ISAPI extension, and facilitating the transfer of control of a request to an arbitrary URL (albeit one in the same application pool), and to incorporate the output of one or more arbitrary URLs into its response. Additionally, vectored buffer transmission and the ability for an ISAPI application to report itself unhealthy and to request a recycle have been added in IIS 6.0.

With that covered, let's take a look at the new features and improvements in IIS 6.0 in terms of what they bring to the table: Security, Reliability, Performance, and Administration.

Security

Microsoft has taken a much more active role in the securing of servers, and IIS 6.0 stands out as an example of that new stance. Adopting a position of "lockdown" as the default, when Windows Server 2003 is installed, IIS 6.0 is not included in the default installation. This prevents the scenarios where the administrators, unaware that IIS had been installed, did not take any steps to secure the data on the server. This helped attackers to compromise the security and integrity of the server data. Furthermore, after IIS6.0 is explicitly installed, all services except the requests for static web pages are disabled by default; and must be specifically enabled. This ensures that the administrators consciously choose which services (ASP, CGI, ASP.NET) to enable.

"Locked Down" server

Taking the "less is more" approach further, IIS 6.0 is initially configured such that only those services that process the requests for static web pages (such as .htm, .gif or .jpg) are enabled by default, and all other services must be specifically enabled. For all requests to features that are not enabled, a generic 404 Not Found message is returned. To the client, it appears as if the requested file or service is simply not available, reducing the amount of potentially useful information given to an attacker. This is referred to as the "lockdown" state. While denying this detailed information to potential attackers, IIS 6.0 had added a "logging subcode" to the web activity logs, making the actual reason for the 404 Not Found message clear to the administrators.

Many features such as FrontPage Server Extensions, ISAPI, and CGI processing, which were previously enabled by default, are now disabled when IIS is initially installed, and have to be specifically enabled. New features are also disabled by default, and can be enabled from the **Web Service Extensions** configuration page in the IIS Manager.

Advanced Digest Authentication

Advanced Digest Authentication is a new user authentication scheme for clients who want to access the server. The administrator can set this authentication scheme for web sites so that only the users with the correct username and password are allowed. With Advanced Digest Authentication, user credentials sent over the network are now packaged and stored locally as an MD5 hash; this makes it much more difficult to derive a user's password, even if the credentials are intercepted during transmission or retrieved from the web server. MD5 is an algorithm that takes an input and produces a 128-bit "fingerprint" or "message digest", unique to the input. For more information on MD5, refer to http://www.rfc-editor.org/rfc/rfc1321.txt.

FTP User Isolation

FTP User Isolation allows each FTP site to specify its own, separate directory, which will appear and act as the root directory for that site. In other words, users will not be able to navigate to a directory above the specified root directory, and thereby traverse to other directories that they should not see and have much less access for.

While user isolation is new to IIS 6.0, all other FTP functionality, including creating and deleting files and directories, works as it did in previous versions of IIS.

Selectable Worker Process Identity

IIS 6.0 allows for multiple **application pools**, which is an obvious improvement over IIS 5, which allowed only one application pool. Each application pool has its own security identity under which it runs. This allows each application pool to run under an account having the minimum level of permissions needed to accomplish its tasks.

In many cases, a web server may host multiple sites, often for multiple groups, divisions, or even companies. In this case, it is imperative that not only each site be isolated from others but that the administrative interfaces for that site be isolated as well. By selecting different security identities for each application pool, it is possible to ensure that the privileges granted to one web site do not overlap with those granted to another.

Secure Sockets Layer

SSL 3.0 provides both a secure channel between a client and a server as well as a mechanism for the server to identify the client. IIS 6.0 improves upon the performance of SSL, with a new streamlined implementation. For administrators who must manage hundreds (if not thousands) of IIS servers with SSL certificates, the new **CertObject**, allows for the remote management of SSL certificates.

Selectable Cryptographic Service Provider

The cryptography functions required for SSL are a drain on performance as they are processor intensive. IIS 6.0 allows for the specification of a specific cryptographic service provider, such as those available with dedicated encryption hardware designed to improve performance as well as security. As all cryptographic providers implement identical methods of the **Cryptography Application Programming Interface (CryptoAPI)**, they are interchangeable without the need to modify web application code. We will look at these security features in greater detail in *Chapter 3*.

Reliability

When creating web applications for reliability, good code can only go so far – and sometimes legacy applications have problems that can't be readily fixed. When it comes to reliability, the web server must be both the first as well as the last line of defence. A web server must be fault tolerant, able to recognize problems, and shut down or restart as necessary, whilst also maintaining the ability to queue new incoming requests until a new process is started.

IIS 6.0 provides improved reliability through a number of architectural changes, the most notable being a new isolation environment that creates separate, isolated processes for web applications. Applications are executed within a user mode process called **worker process**. A worker process is the host process, and all applications are loaded and run in its context. A worker process receives request from the HTTP listener (HTTP.sys), and processes and replies to those requests. The worker processes executes in an isolated environment, where each worker process is separated from others by operating system process boundaries.

Through this new Worker Process Isolation Mode, the worker processes are placed in **application pools**, which are individually configurable collections of processes. An Application pool is essentially a group of applications that share one worker process. It is represented by a request queue, which accepts requests for applications in that group. An application pool may share more than one worker process. Application pools allow for finer control of resources by enabling control over configuration parameters such as request queue lengths, timeouts, bandwidth usage, and connection limits.

Kernel-mode HTTP listener

IIS 6.0 now relies upon a kernel-mode HTTP driver, HTTP.sys, for queuing and processing HTTP requests. HTTP.sys is an integral part of the Windows Server 2003 network stack, and serves all applications that require HTTP services (not just IIS). Being a separate kernel mode driver, HTTP.sys does not allow for any application-specific code to be loaded into its process, removing the possibility of crashing due to bad user code.

HTTP.sys creates queues for each application pool, listening for HTTP requests and placing those requests in the appropriate queue based on the URI namespace of the request. In previous versions of IIS, a server crash would mean that all requests were either ignored or received an error. In IIS 6.0, should an application pool crash or experience a scheduled recycle, requests remain in the queue until the application pool has restarted and is ready to accept them.

Connection management and bandwidth throttling allows you to limit the bandwidth used by IIS to ensure that resources are available for other services such as e-mail, or for other sites on the same machine. Previous versions of IIS provided limited bandwidth throttling on a server-wide basis. IIS 6.0 now allows more application-specific configuration of these **Quality-of-Service (QoS)** features by separating applications into individually configurable application pools. Each application pool's configuration information is presented to HTTP.sys to ensure that the kernel-mode driver takes it into account while processing requests.

Web Administration Service

With HTTP.sys on the front-end and application pools on the other end, the **Web Administration Service (WAS)** could be said to be "watching over it all". WAS is responsible for configuration management and also the configuration and monitoring of application pools and worker processes. Like HTTP.sys the WAS does not allow for the loading of third-party code, protecting its process space from potential user-introduced bugs.

WAS processes the configuration metabase and configures HTTP.sys to listen for requests based on the URI namespaces served by each application pool. This instructs HTTP.sys to begin to accept requests for each application pool. Then HTTP.sys starts a worker process to service requests for that pool. WAS is also responsible for determining the life cycle of worker processes, including startup, shutdown, and recycling.

Health and Crash Monitoring

In worker process isolation mode, worker processes are constantly monitored, via a mechanism known as **pinging,** for malfunctions or other problems, enabling corrective action to be taken such as restarting the worker process. WAS checks worker processes periodically to ensure that they are running properly. Should a worker process experience a problem (such as being blocked due to a hung connection and unable to take requests) WAS will terminate the worker process and restart it.

Idle Timeout

Application pools that have not been used in a configurable amount of time can be shut down, thereby conserving system resources. Any request received for a shutdown application pool would restart it as needed.

Rapid Fail Protection

Repeated failures of an application pool can signal IIS 6.0 to disable that pool until corrective action can be taken. Part of WAS's monitoring strategy is to notice when the communication channel with a worker process is lost, indicating a failure of that worker process. Under normal circumstances, a failure would result in the restart of the worker process. **Rapid Fail Protection** disables applications that suffer multiple, repeated failures in a certain period of time, causing HTTP.sys to return 503 Service Unavailable responses when a request is received for the URL namespace of the web application that was shut down.

Demand Start

IIS 6.0 has the ability to listen for requests for a large number of sites, yet not need a worker process to be ready for every site. If a request is received for a site that does not have a worker process currently running, IIS 6.0 will "demand start" the process to serve the request. Combined with the ability to timeout unused worker processes, this provides IIS 6.0 with the ability to serve more sites than would be feasible if they were all active simultaneously. Additionally, IIS will dynamically scale the HTTP.sys kernel caching of sites that are idle providing more cache space for active applications.

Process Recycling

Worker processes can be restarted as per a pre-determined schedule, which allows the management of applications with problems such as memory leaks. Restarts may be scheduled based on elapsed time, requests, memory usage, or on a pre-determined schedule. Through administrative tools, a recycle may be requested at any time on demand. This feature is especially useful in cases where the application source code is not available, precluding actually fixing the problem.

When a process is restarted, WAS sets a time limit for the existing worker process to complete its shutdown. If that time limit is exceeded, WAS will force the process to shut down. At the same time a new process is started and HTTP.sys is informed of the new process, eliminating any interruptions in service. Within the timeframe of the limit imposed by WAS, the old worker process is allowed to "drain" the queue. That is, the existing worker process completes any outstanding queued requests. The new request architecture and related features will be described in *Chapter 2*.

Performance and Scalability

Being able to serve more requests, and serve them faster, is the basis for server performance, and is always a key goal in any server scenario. Better performance means more clients can be serviced with less physical hardware. This translates directly to greater capacity and cost savings as new equipment purchases can be pushed back while existing equipment finds new life due to better-performing server software.

Performance Implications of HTTP.sys

Without doubt, the key performance improvement in IIS 6.0 (and Windows Server 2003) is the kernel mode HTTP listener, HTTP.sys. It creates queues for each application pool, listening for HTTP requests and placing those requests in the appropriate queue based on the URI namespace of the request. If the response is static, HTTP.sys will respond from its URI based kernel-mode cache. This allows static data to be served from the cache without ever making a processor transition from kernel to user mode, which takes up processor cycles and thereby affects performance. IIS monitors requests and determines its caching strategy based on a new heuristic that takes into account the distribution of requests over time.

If the data is not in the cache, HTTP.sys routes the request to the appropriate user mode worker process without the need to involve any other user mode application. Should a worker process crash or experience a scheduled recycle, requests remain in the queue until the worker process has restarted and is ready to accept them, again without the need for any user mode intervention.

Worker Process Isolation

Earlier versions of IIS ran web application code in-process with the web server, or routed requests to out-of-process applications. With IIS 6.0, each web application is contained within one or more worker processes, eliminating the concept of in-process user code, and completely removing user code from core web server processes.

This new isolation means that while failures in a worker process will not impact on other worker processes on the same machine, they also do not suffer the performance impacts of previous out-of-process modes. Requests come directly from HTTP.sys to the appropriate worker process, eliminating costly process transitions. Additionally, web applications can now be managed, even removed, without the need to shut down the web service. Management tasks such as taking an application offline or online (both manually as well as at scheduled times), resource allocation, performance monitoring, and debugging can be accomplished on an individual worker process without impacting on other worker processes or the server as a whole.

IIS 5 Isolation Mode

IIS 6.0 provides for backward compatibility in cases where web applications cannot be quickly or easily ported to IIS 6.0's new **Worker Process Isolation Mode** (see section *Reliability*), due to problems with multiple instances or non-supported features like read raw filters. In these cases, IIS may be run in IIS 5 Isolation Mode.

Unlike Worker Process Isolation Mode, IIS 5 isolation mode maintains the isolation modes present in IIS 5: low, medium (pooled), and high.

One benefit that is passed on, however, is the kernel-mode HTTP listener; that is, both modes benefit from queuing and caching within the kernel. The isolation modes are explained in detail in *Chapter 2*.

Web Gardens

IIS 6.0 Worker Process Isolation Mode allows you to create multiple application pools, each having its own separate configuration, serving one or more web applications. As the worker processes in application pools communicate directly with HTTP.sys, performance improvements are realized by eliminating the middle layers that would require more process transitions.

By default, each application pool has only one worker process. When more than one worker process resides within an application pool, then that application pool is said to be a "**Web Garden**". Much like a "**Web Farm**" is comprised of two or more separate servers for the same web application, a Web Garden implements this idea within a single server. Requests for a web application are routed to the worker processes within a Web Garden by HTTP.sys in a round-robin fashion. Web Gardens are an especially good solution in the case of a multi-processor machine, where the multiple worker processes may have their processor affinity configured to run on individual processors.

With multiple worker processes, if one process becomes unresponsive, other worker processes are available to process requests. Planned recycling of worker processes in a Web Garden is also done in a round-robin fashion, ensuring that only one worker process is being recycled at a time.

Asynchronous CGI

Common Gateway Interface (CGI) requests are implemented asynchronously in IIS 6.0, eliminating situations where a CGI request could block other responses.

ASP Caching

Active Server Pages (ASP) now caches templates containing ASP scripts and returns cached data without the need for a re-compile. This feature is known as the **Persisted ASP Template Cache**, and by default stores 250 templates in its in-memory cache. Whereas IIS 5 would remove older compiled templates from memory as newer ones were added, IIS 6.0 will begin to cache to disk should the in-memory cache be filled, preventing a possibly costly recompile.

Administration

Managing web servers and groups of servers (Web Farms) has become more complex. No longer is management simply a process of modifying a single configuration file and occasionally restarting a server. Today's web application environment requires robust management capabilities, remote administration services, complex and thorough logging facilities, and the ability to examine, evaluate and maintain every aspect of a server, from global performance settings to the smallest individual component. IIS 6.0 includes many additions and enhancements to the tools available to administrators to accomplish these tasks.

Command-Line Administration

IIS 6.0 ships with a set of command-line administration scripts for the management of the server, the majority of which are new and created using the new **Windows Management Instrumentation (WMI)** provider for IIS. This provides more complete support for IIS 6.0 than the existing **Active Directory Services Interface (ADSI)** provider. Tasks such as the creation, deleting, starting, and stopping of web sites, FTP sites, virtual directories, and applications are accomplished through these scripts, without the need for a user interface. Additionally, IIS configuration data may be imported, exported, backed up, and restored through the command-line scripts. These scripts are also an excellent way to learn how to use the new WMI provider for IIS 6.0.

Command-Line Script	Purpose
iisweb.vbs	Create, delete, start, stop, and list web sites
iisftp.vbs	Create, delete, start, stop, and list FTP sites
iisvdir.vbs	Create and delete virtual directories (Web)
iisftpdr.vbs	Create, delete, and display virtual directories (FTP)
iiscnfg.vbs	Export and import IIS configuration data (XML)
iisback.vbs	Backup and restore IIS configurations

The details of the tools and services available for administering IIS 6.0 can be found in *Chapter 4*.

Logging

More than one site can now write to a centralized binary log thereby improving performance by eliminating the need for IIS to format logging data, as it must do for all other logging types. With binary logging, the raw data is placed into the database directly. Furthermore, by using a database, multiple web servers may combine their logs into a single, centralized location. IIS 6.0 also supports IIS, NCSA, and W3C Extended logging formats.

IIS 6.0 supports logging in **UTF-8** as well as the local code page, allowing information to be stored in languages other than English. The various logging formats and the settings involved to use these features can be found in *Chapter 6*.

Development

IIS 6.0 provides new features from the development perspective, aimed at helping developers create better-performing and more reliable applications for the Web. An application can now be configured so that when the application faults, it is left in a state in which a debugger can be started and attached to the application. New features introduced in ISAPI allow for implementing the functionality of ISAPI filters into extensions, thus combining the advantages of both ISAPI components.

Orphan Worker Processes

Normally, a worker process that is malfunctioning (or has crashed outright) would be terminated and restarted. Rather than shutting down a failing worker process, it is possible to configure IIS 6.0 to separate failing worker processes such that a debugger may be attached to the process for diagnostics. The process, known as "orphaning" a worker process, is controlled by WAS, and results in the malfunctioning worker process being left in its running state. WAS can then run a pre-configured command, perhaps starting a debugger.

IIS WMI Provider

Windows Server 2003 includes the WMI provider, first introduced in Windows 2000. WMI is functionally equivalent to ADSI, while providing an extensible schema, query support, associations between objects, and access to other information like performance counters and system configuration. IIS 6.0 includes a WMI provider, which offers more powerful and configurable administrative programming interfaces based on the extensible nature of WMI.

ISAPI

IIS 6.0 continues to enhance the feature set of ISAPI, with new functionality for custom errors, vectored buffer and file handle transmission, Unicode support, and a new strategy for internal redirection.

Custom Errors

The HSE_REQ_SEND_CUSTOM_ERROR server support function allows ISAPI developers to utilize the custom error support built in to IIS 6.0, rather than having to create their own custom errors.

VectorSend

The HSE_REQ_VECTORSEND server support function allows ISAPI applications to transmit groups of buffers or file handles as a single response; thus eliminating the need to performing multiple WriteClient operations (and the transition from user to kernel mode each time), or to combine a lot of data into a single, unified buffer (and the memory it requires). VectorSend takes a list of buffers or file handles and allows HTTP.sys to assemble and transmit the response from within kernel mode.

Unicode Support

As Unicode becomes more pervasive, and UTF-8 encoded URLs are seen more often, ISAPI allows developers to access server variables in Unicode as well as access the Unicode version of a URL.

ExecuteURL

The new (and recommended) method for internal redirection is now through the HSE_REQ_EXEC_URL server support function, and provides the needed functionality to chain requests.

The real win for ExecuteURL is that, in almost all cases, it is an excellent replacement for read raw data filters. Until now, the only way to examine and modify entity bodies in requests had been through a read raw data notification, meaning that a very difficult to create ISAPI filter (which often did not function as expected) had to be developed. ISAPI extensions provide an easier platform upon which to manipulate entity bodies, and then pass them to a child request.

Reporting Unhealthy

The HSE_REQ_REPORT_UNHEALTHY server support function allows an ISAPI extension to report that its worker process requires recycling. ISAPI developers can use this function in cases where their ISAPI extension suffers an error that a recycle might resolve, or enters an unstable state. A string may be passed along with this function to be included in the event log entry for the worker process recycle.

Wildcard Application Mappings (Global Interceptors)

Global Interceptors allow an ISAPI application to be run for every request to a web site or virtual directory. They provide the ability to change, redirect, or even deny requests to a particular URL namespace. Whereas IIS 5 allowed for one wildcard scriptmap, IIS 6.0 now allows multiple Global Interceptors.

Global Interceptors, unlike the functionality in IIS 5, are ISAPI extensions. Previously, only ISAPI filters could implement this functionality. This had a number of disadvantages including the fact that filters are global for the entire web site (as opposed to being limited to a particular URL namespace), cannot access the entity body of the request, and cannot run for extended periods of time without depleting the IIS thread pool.

Combined with the functionality of ExecuteURL, there are practically no scenarios where an ISAPI filter is the indicated solution in IIS 6.0. ISAPI components will be discussed in detail in *Chapter 7*.

New Features

IIS 6.0 allows ASP applications to use **COM+** components more easily than in IIS 5. The most significant feature of IIS 6.0 is the use of XML to store configuration data in the metabase, and edit it while the server is running without the need for restarting. This entails all advantages of XML and allows better management of configuration data. IIS 6.0 supports IPv6, thereby ensuring your server is ready for the future of the Internet.

COM+ Services

In IIS 5, ASP applications used **COM+** services by configuring the application's **Web Application Manager** (**WAM**) object, as the COM+ components were designed to be used with COM components. IIS 6.0 separates COM+ services from components, allowing ASP applications to use a set of COM+ services more easily.

ASP supports **Fusion**, allowing ASP applications to use specific versions of system DLLs or COM components based on application needs. Previously, applications would use whichever version of a DLL or COM object that was present on the system, often causing problems when a new version was installed with unexpected functionality. We will learn more about COM+ services in IIS 6.0 in *Chapter 8*.

XML Metabase

The IIS 6.0 metabase is an XML file containing configuration data for all aspects of IIS. Previous versions of IIS used a proprietary, binary metabase file (MetaBase.bin), which was not directly readable with a text editor. IIS 6.0 now features a text-based XML metabase, which can be edited directly (in the editor) as well as using a programmatic interface. The metabase itself is stored in an XML text file called MetaBase.xml, and the schema, containing all of the default values, is located in an XML file called MBSchema.xml.

While IIS maintains its copy of the metabase information in the memory, the metabase can be edited while IIS is running, and will import changes as they are saved. The metabase can literally be edited using a text editor like Notepad while IIS is running. Performance enhancements include a faster load than previous versions and smaller disk usage.

The metabase also supports automatic history file creation and versioning, allowing you to roll back to a previous version, by maintaining copies of each version of the metabase as changes are saved. When a new version of the metabase is saved, the previous version is assigned a version number higher than that of the last saved copy in the history folder, which can be used for rollback in the case of problems.

The metabase supports exporting and importing of individual nodes, allowing for the quick replication of configuration information between sites and machines. Exports and backups of the metabase may be made in a machine-independent manner as well, facilitating the copy of metabase information across multiple machines. Backups contain complete images of the metabase, while exporting may contain only selected portions of the metabase. Backups can be saved with a password, which is used to encrypt the session key of the backup. This allows the backup to be restored to another computer by decrypting the session key with the administrator-supplied password, and then re-encrypting it with the machine key.

Programmatic access to the metabase is accomplished through the **Admin Base Object** (**ABO**) interface. ABO exposes metabase information as a number of COM object interfaces. All relevant discussion on the XML metabase is provided in *Chapter 4*.

IPv6

IIS 6.0 provides support for the next generation of the **Internet Protocol version 6** (**IPv6**). Windows Server 2003 ships with IPv6 support, but it should be noted that, for IIS 6.0, IPv6 support is limited. Specifically, IPv6 support is enabled for all sites or none – there is no per-site configuration option. SSL support for IPv6 is limited to a single SSL site per computer due to IP routing restrictions. When using IPv6, only host header routing is supported. Bandwidth throttling, site routing based on IP address, and reverse DNS lookups are not supported with IPv6.

IIS supports IPv6 in ISAPI applications by providing IPv6 responses in local and remote host server variables (LOCAL_ADDR and REMOTE_ADDR) when connecting clients are using IPv6. Log files will have IPv6 addresses logged when available.

Summary

This chapter provided an overview of IIS 6.0 and briefly discussed many of its new features in the areas of security, reliability, performance, scalability, administration, and development. Microsoft has made quite a few changes to the architecture and functionality provided by IIS, to ensure an improved capability for both the administrators and developers. This chapter attempted to provide a quick look at them, before they are described in detail in the chapters to come.

IIS 6

Programming

Handbook

2

The New Request Architecture

In the earliest versions of IIS, web application code ran in-process within the web server itself, and unloading or replacing an application often meant restarting the entire web service. It also meant that if an application had problems, it typically took IIS down with it. Even worse was that errors in a web application could end up corrupting other web applications. Starting with IIS 4, support for out-of-process applications was introduced. However, this meant performance degradation as requests were first sent to the main IIS process, then to the out-of-process application, and finally back to the main IIS process again. With the release of IIS 6.0, the entire underlying request processing architecture has been redesigned and vastly improved over previous versions, improving both reliability as well as performance.

In IIS 6.0, the components that are critical to the proper functioning of web services are isolated from all web applications. All requests are handled by the kernel-mode HTTP handler **HTTP.sys**. All applications that process the requests are handled by the **Web Administration Service (WAS)**. All web applications now run out-of-process, but without the performance penalty, as the requests are routed to the appropriate process directly from HTTP.sys. The HTTP.sys and the WAS, reside in their own separate process spaces and do not allow third-party code to be loaded into them, preventing a misbehaving web application from affecting the web services.

IIS 6.0 has the capability to isolate third-party code into separate **application pools** of one or more **worker processes**, to avoid impacting the entire server when an application malfunctions.

A **worker process** is simply a user mode application, which processes HTTP requests such as requests for a static page, invoking an ISAPI filter or extension, running a CGI, or executing application code. Worker processes are implemented as executables called w3wp.exe and are controlled by WAS. The HTTP.sys listener routes requests and responses to and from worker processes.

An **application pool** is a group of web applications that share one or more worker processes. Application pools allow configuration information to be applied separately to one or more web applications and the worker processes that serve them. Each application within an application pool shares one or more worker processes.

With this new architecture, IIS 6.0 automatically detects application crashes, memory leaks, and other errors. When these conditions occur, IIS 6.0 provides fault tolerance as well as the ability to restart the worker processes as necessary. IIS 6.0 also takes the preventive step of recycling worker processes, thereby avoiding memory leaks and performance degradations before they build up. In these cases, IIS 6.0 continues to queue requests without interrupting the user experience.

In this chapter, we will examine the features and components of the new request architecture, and discuss the following topics:

- Request flow architecture
- Application Isolation Modes
- Kernel-mode HTTP listener (HTTP.sys)
- Web Administration Service (WAS)
- Application Pools
- Application Health Monitoring
- Web Gardens

Request Flow Architecture

We will now take a look at how a request is processed and what path it follows within IIS. The path of the request has been illustrated in the following diagram:

Figure 1

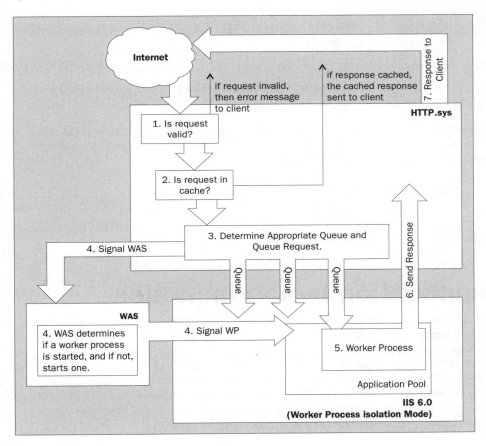

The request flow occurs as follows:

1. When a request arrives, `HTTP.sys` determines if the request is initially valid. If it is not, an Invalid Request error code is sent back to the client and the connection is closed.

2. If the request is valid, `HTTP.sys` then checks to see if the response can be found in its kernel mode cache and, if it is present in the cache, `HTTP.sys` sends the response.

3. If the response is not in the cache, HTTP.sys then determines the appropriate application pool to receive the request, and puts the request into that application pool's request queue. All processing up to this point is handled in the kernel mode.

4. If there is no worker process running for the queue, HTTP.sys notifies WAS to start a worker process. WAS is the first user mode application becoming involved in the process.

5. Worker processes check their queues, and pick up the requests that are waiting for processing.

6. After processing, the worker process sends the response back to HTTP.sys

7. HTTP.sys sends the response back to the client and, if configured to do so, logs the request.

We will describe the key components, HTTP.sys and WAS, and their roles in the request path flow, later in the chapter. However, before that we need to understand the isolation modes offered by IIS 6.0:

❑ **Worker Process Isolation Mode**

❑ **IIS 5 Isolation Mode**

All applications are executed in either one of the two modes.

Application Isolation Modes

While both modes still use HTTP.sys as their listener, they are distinctly different in their operation. The isolation mode you select will have an impact on both performance and reliability, and will determine which features are available to you. Worker Process Isolation Mode is the recommended mode of operation for IIS 6.0, as it offers increased reliability through better isolation of applications. You should use worker process isolation mode unless there is a genuine issue of compatibility that will force you to use IIS 5 isolation mode; such as the need for **ISAPI raw read filters**, a feature that is not supported in worker process isolation mode.

IIS 6.0 Worker Processes Isolation Mode

The new IIS 6.0 mode is called **Worker Process Isolation Mode**, because all applications are isolated as worker processes and hosted by a **Web Application Manager (WAM)** object, instead of dllhost.exe, as in previous versions. In IIS 5.0, you were limited to a single application pool. In IIS 6.0, you may have many application pools of worker processes, each worker process being an instance of an application called w3wp.exe. You might think of each worker process as its own **World Wide Web Publishing Service (W3SVC)**, able to load and host applications in-process. In essence, anything that was done in W3SVC (in IIS 5) is now done by the worker processes in IIS 6.0.

How Worker Process Isolation Mode works

IIS 6.0 creates a separate worker process for each application pool, configuring each application to work in a separate isolated process, and thus ensuring that applications do not interfere with each other. An ISAPI application that would have crashed in IIS 5, would have taken down the whole server. In IIS 6.0 worker process isolation mode, such a crash would be detected and handled, with the rest of the server completely unharmed by any problem. The WAS doesn't restart worker processes until there's a request for the web application, thereby preserving resources until a worker process is actually needed.

The following diagram illustrates the working of worker process isolation mode:

Figure 2

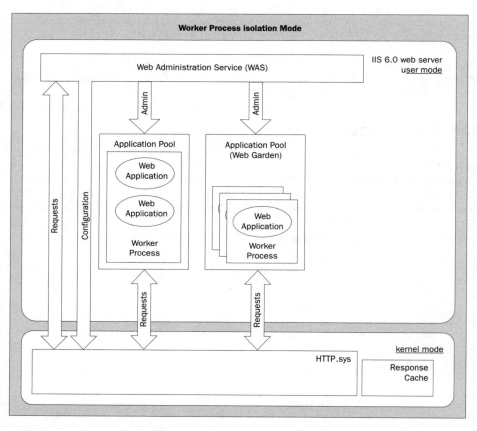

HTTP.sys resides in kernel mode. In user mode, WAS manages application pools and the configuration of both HTTP.sys as well as application pools.

The Benefits of Worker Process Isolation Mode

IIS 6.0 Worker Process Isolation Mode improves upon the previous process models by providing increased scalability, reliability, and manageability. In this mode, there can be multiple worker processes available to handle requests, and each worker process is multi-threaded and capable of handling multiple user requests.

With multiple worker processes, **Web Gardens** can be created, further increasing scalability on multi-processor machines. Like a **Web Farm**, which is comprised of a number of similar machines working to balance request loads, a Web Garden is a single machine, balancing request loads across multiple processors. The key difference in IIS 6.0 is that worker processes can be assigned to individual processors. This way, if a worker process is blocked for a period of time, on a request that takes time (such as a database query), other worker processes are available on other processors. Worker process recycling may be configured to occur on a round-robin basis between processors, eliminating the short downtime during a recycle.

With all user code removed from the HTTP listener and WAS, IIS 6.0 provides increased reliability through isolation of potentially harmful code. Additionally, application health monitoring ensures that malfunctioning or misbehaving code is recycled or shut down gracefully as appropriate. Grouping similarly configured applications into application pools allows for better control over configuration, increasing manageability, and allows for control down to the namespace/application level.

IIS 5.0 Isolation Mode

There are a number of reasons that the new worker process isolation mode may not be right for you. Your application may not be able to operate when there are multiple instances running, or may not be able to deal with the possible conditions in which the session state may be lost. While both of these issues can be addressed with configuration changes in worker process isolation mode, an insurmountable problem is that in many cases there are existing applications that make use of ISAPI's read raw data feature, which does not work in IIS 6.0 worker process isolation mode.

If you do not intend to upgrade to the new way of doing things, you will want to use **IIS 5.0 Isolation Mode**, which provides backwards compatibility for applications that require an environment similar to IIS 5. As in IIS 5, applications run as part of IIS process (in-process, inside of `inetinfo.exe`) or in separate process (`dllhost.exe`), but there is no isolation between web applications. `HTTP.sys` processes requests for this mode in the same way as IIS 6.0 worker process isolation mode.

The following diagram illustrates the working of IIS 5 isolation mode:

Figure 3

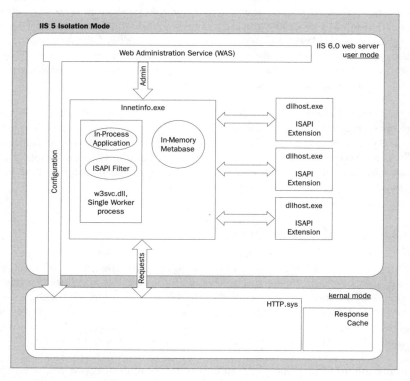

In the previous diagram, note the absence of all but one worker process. In this mode, HTTP.sys creates only one request queue. This was the drawback of IIS 5 isolation mode in that it provided only one application pool.

Which Mode?

IIS 6.0 will initialize itself in either worker process isolation mode or IIS 5 isolation mode, but not both. In other words, it is not possible to run some web applications in worker process isolation mode and others in IIS 5 isolation mode. New installations of IIS 6.0 will start in IIS 6.0 worker process isolation mode, while upgrades of any older versions of IIS (including version 5 and below) will start in IIS 5.0 isolation mode by default. Upgrades from IIS 6.0 will retain the mode previously used. If in the process of an upgrade, the mode is switched to worker process isolation mode, all applications will be placed in the single default application pool. Note that when the applications are so moved, their isolation configuration will be different from their previous configuration, and may need to be manually changed. See the section *Application Isolation and Performance* later in the chapter.

Switching Between Modes

You can change the application isolation mode, either with the **Microsoft Management Console** (**MMC**) snap-in or the scripting interfaces, and you can change it back and forth at any time. For example, if you are running an application that uses read raw filters, you can set the mode to IIS 5 isolation mode while you redesign your application. Once the redesign is done, you can set it back to worker process isolation mode. The application isolation mode is controlled through the `IIS5IsolationModeEnabled` property in the metabase (the IIS 6.0 configuration data structure). Setting this property to false will enable worker process isolation mode, and setting it to true will enable IIS 5 isolation mode. Changing this value requires a restart of the W3SVC service before the change is enacted.

You can change the isolation mode by starting the **IIS Manager** and accessing the Properties for web sites. The mode can be set in the property page under the Service tab:

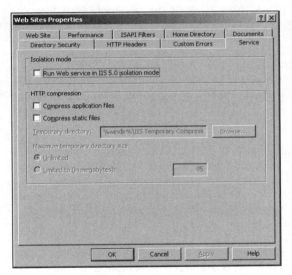

Architectural Considerations of Worker Process Isolation Mode

There are a number of considerations to keep in mind when designing applications (or porting and configuring existing applications) for worker process isolation mode. State management becomes more complicated in an environment where processes may be recycled, as one process may be shut down in favor of a new one. Processes may be running multiple times, which adds new challenges for applications that must be prepared to operate in a multi-instanced environment. Worker process isolation mode also presents changes to the way that ISAPI filters operate, including the absence of read raw filters. We'll also take a look at special considerations for ASP.NET, and the implications of application isolation on performance.

State Management

When a worker process times out due to idle processing and is automatically shut down, any session state information stored in that process may be lost. Recycling, which causes the worker process to be restarted, may result in lost state as well. Applications should persist any state externally (such as in a database, or the ASP.NET session service). If your session state management code cannot be modified, IIS should be configured to run in a mode that does not threaten to lose state, including disabling recycling and idle timeout of worker processes.

Multi-Instancing

Multi-instancing, or two or more instances of a process running simultaneously, can pose problems for applications not prepared for this occurrence. Applications that use kernel objects such as mutexes, must be prepared for other instances to be accessing the same object, both within the same process as well as other processes. Applications that implement custom logging modules must be prepared for other instances to be accessing the same log. To avoid multi-instancing issues, you will not only need to ensure that there is only one worker process per application pool, but you will also need to disable overlapped recycling, which could result in the existence of two worker processes during the overlapped portion of an application pool recycle.

ISAPI Filters

In IIS 5.0, ISAPI filters ran in `inetinfo.exe` as LocalSystem and were guaranteed to be single-instanced. In worker process isolation mode, this is no longer the case. ISAPI filters may be multi-instanced, have different process identities, and are subject to recycling. Perhaps most importantly, the worker process isolation mode does not support `SF_READ_RAW_DATA` and `SF_SEND_RAW_DATA`. If you have a filter that registers for these notifications, and cannot be modified, you will have to run in IIS 5 isolation mode.

To resolve these issues in IIS 6.0, it is recommended that you use ISAPI extensions instead of filters. With the addition of wildcard scriptmaps and the `HSE_REQ_EXEC_URL` server support function, ISAPI extensions may now be used in the same role as traditional ISAPI filters. Additionally, ISAPI extensions are asynchronous (as opposed to the synchronous nature of ISAPI filters), which will provide significant performance gains. For more information on filters and extensions, see *Chapter 7*.

Special considerations for ASP.NET

ASP.NET was originally released for use with IIS 5.0 and used its own process model. When ASP.NET is run in IIS 5 isolation mode, it will use its own process model and configuration settings as provided in the `machine.config` file. When ASP.NET runs on IIS 6.0, however, it uses the worker process isolation mode, disabling its own process model. This means that if your ASP.NET application has specific configuration settings in the `<processModel>` section of its `machine.config` file, most of those settings will be ignored in favor of the worker process isolation mode settings. The exceptions to this rule are the `maxIOThreads` and `maxWorkerThreads` entries, which will be read and used by IIS. The `maxIOThreads` value will control the number of threads the worker process will use to receive asynchronous requests from `HTTP.sys`, and the `maxWorkerThreads` value will set the number of application threads used by the ASP.NET ISAPI.

Application Isolation and Performance

Not to be confused with the concept of application isolation modes, **application isolation** is the separation of applications by process boundaries, which prevents them from interfering with one another. As we have seen, application isolation in worker process isolation mode is accomplished via application pools. In IIS 5 isolation mode, you can configure isolation using the `AppIsolated` property setting for the application, selecting in-process, pooled, or high isolation. This is very similar to the options available to you in IIS 5.0. In either pooled or high isolation mode, there is a performance hit caused by remote procedure calls necessary between `inetinfo` and the WAM object (an example of which would be retrieving an ISAPI Server Variable). This performance hit is not present in worker process isolation mode, as applications are loaded in-process to `w3wp.exe`.

Here's a comparison between the two modes with respect to the features provided:

Feature	Worker Process Isolation Mode	IIS 5 Isolation Mode
Basic Request/Response	Yes	Yes
Runs ISAPI Filters and ISAPI Extensions	Yes, as Worker Processes	Yes, In-process (`inetinfo.exe`) as well as out-of-process (`dllhost.exe`)
Worker Process Management	Yes, in WAS. Processes run as `w3wp.exe`	No
Application Pooling	Yes (multiple pools)	Limited (one pool only)
Application Recycling	Yes	No

Feature	Worker Process Isolation Mode	IIS 5 Isolation Mode
Web Gardens	Yes	No
Health Monitoring	Yes	No
Debugging	Yes	Limited
Processor Affinity	Yes	No
Performance Tuning	Yes	Limited
HTTP.sys Configuration	Yes, in WAS	Yes, in WAS
Out-of-Process ISAPI	w3wp.exe	dllhost.exe
ISAPI Filters	w3wp.exe	inetinfo.exe
FTP, NNTP, and SMTP	inetinfo.exe	inetinfo.exe

Now that we have taken a comprehensive look at the isolation modes offered by IIS 6.0, we will describe the two components of the request architecture: HTTP.sys and Web Administration Service.

HTTP.sys

The **Hyper Text Transfer Protocol** (**HTTP**) stack (HTTP.sys) is a new kernel mode driver, listening directly at the TCP/IP level, and is the sole channel for HTTP requests to IIS. In IIS 5, HTTP requests were served by the **Winsock/afd.sys** components, which had difficulty sharing ownership of port 80, the port for HTTP and port 443, the port for **Secure Socket Layers** (**SSL**). Furthermore, since there were several teams at Microsoft who all implemented their own version of the HTTP server-side stack, there were a number of places where bugs could be introduced into the HTTP process.

For Windows Server 2003 (which includes the IIS 6.0), the networking team decided to unify those efforts and develop a server-side HTTP listener that would offer a pure "request and response" kernel mode API. **Kernel mode** describes the privileged processor mode in which the NT-based operating system executive code runs. The code executing in the kernel mode has access to critical operating system resources, such as system memory and hardware. The boundary between kernel mode and **user mode** (in which applications run) is designed to protect the operating system from bugs introduced by user code. In other words, a misbehaving application in user mode will not interfere with the operating system or its ability to support other applications.

HTTP.sys is a new part of the networking subsystem in Windows Server 2003, and is available not only to IIS 6.0, but also other components as well. Having a separate HTTP service allows other applications that utilize HTTP to benefit from a dedicated high-performance HTTP stack. HTTP.sys is responsible for all TCP connection management, request routing, text-based logging, caching, and **Quality-of-Service (QoS)** functions, including bandwidth management, connection limits and timeouts, and queue length limits. Since HTTP.sys is not processing requests other than routing them to the correct consumer, no application-specific code is ever loaded into the kernel mode. This means that developers don't need to worry about errors being introduced into the kernel mode that cause an appearance of the dreaded blue screen.

Kernel-level Queuing

HTTP requests come into HTTP.sys (which is responsible for all connection management) and are routed to the appropriate application pool by way of a **Universal Resource Identifier (URI)** namespace. Application pools will be covered in detail later – for now, consider an application pool as one or more web applications on your server. Each application pool registers those portions of the URI namespace for which it services requests, and receives its own request queue within HTTP.sys. An application pool may be servicing more than just one portion of the URI namespace.

Since HTTP.sys runs completely within kernel mode, any problems in user mode don't affect it. Even if an application pool has to be restarted (for any reason), HTTP.sys will continue to queue requests for that application pool, anticipating that the pool will recycle and begin to accept requests again. When IIS shuts down, it removes its application pools and their URI namespace registrations from HTTP.sys. This way, while HTTP.sys continues to operate and serve applications other than IIS, it will no longer queue requests for the shutdown IIS application pools.

URI Cache

HTTP.sys implements a URI response cache, allowing it to serve cached responses completely within kernel mode and avoiding a costly transition to user mode. By avoiding the transition from kernel mode to user mode, literally thousands of CPU cycles are cut from each request, and the overall code path to serve a response from the cache is significantly shorter. The mechanism for transitioning to user mode relies on the **Windows IO Manager**, which must acquire, process, and complete IO Request Packets for the transition. This costly procedure is avoided completely when a response is served from the cache, and a performance gain on the order of 100% can be achieved. HTTP.sys has an advanced algorithm for determining what is placed in the cache, basing its decisions on the distribution of requests that a particular application receives.

Quality-of-Service

Quality-of-Service describes the methodology behind managing server resources like memory or CPU cycles. An administrator may control the resources allocated to sites and application pools, thereby affecting the quality of service that other sites and applications receive. Quality-of-Service components include:

❑ **Bandwidth Throttling**

❑ **Connection Limits and Timeouts**

❑ **Application Pool Queue Length Limits**

Bandwidth Throttling

Bandwidth Throttling allows you to limit the amount of bandwidth available to each individual web site. In the case of a server with multiple sites, it often makes sense to limit available bandwidth for non-critical sites and to ensure adequate bandwidth for important sites. As far back as IIS 4, bandwidth throttling could be done on both site and server levels. IIS 6.0 takes advantage of the bandwidth throttling support provided by NT QoS services. With the addition of the `MaxGlobalBandwidth` setting, it is now possible to throttle all sites (that do not have their own individual settings) collectively at a given rate. Sites may have more specific settings, as provided by its individual `MaxBandwidth` setting, which will exclude the site from the global limit.

The bandwidth settings for the server and each web site can be set using the property pages. Open the IIS Manager (enter inetmgr in the Run command window) and right-click the appropriate entry in the left tree structure. That will bring up a menu, where you can click the Properties option and then the Performance tab. That will bring up the following property page:

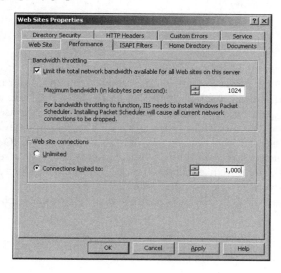

Using the Performance property page, you can configure the bandwidth settings for both the server as well as individual sites.

Connection Limits and Timeouts

Connection Limits, as the name implies, limit the number of simultaneous connections at any one time. If a connection limit is reached, further attempts to connect will receive an error in response, and will then be disconnected. Limits may be set on a per-site basis as well as on the server as a whole. When a connection limit is reached, IIS 6.0 returns a 403.9 error code. In IIS 5, this error was customizable to be a file, URL, or the default text. In IIS 6.0, however, this error is not customizable, and returns the default text only. Connection limits are detected and acted upon from within HTTP.sys. The settings for connection limits can be set using the previous screen as shown.

IIS 6.0 supports four types of connection timeouts. The first three were available in IIS 5, and include a timeout where a connection has sent data but is now idle, a timeout where a connection has been established but no data has been sent, and a timeout on sending a response, based on a minimum bytes-per-second value. The fourth, new to IIS 6.0, is a timeout designed to prevent clients from sending data at an unacceptably slow rate. This ReceiveEntityBody timeout uses the ConnectionTimeout value to ensure that entity bodies are received in a timely manner. Once IIS knows that a request has an entity body, it starts a separate timer for receiving the entity body. This time is reset each time a packet of entity body data is received. If it times out, the connection is closed. The various timeouts provided by IIS 6.0 are:

❑ **ConnectionTimeout**
It specifies the amount of time the server will wait before disconnecting an idle connection. This is similar to the IIS 5 ServerListenTimeout property. In some instances, applications that use port 80 for other tunneling protocols may wish to keep the connection open, even though it is idle. In such cases, this timeout must be increased.

❑ **MinFileBytesPerSec**
It specifies the minimum net bandwidth to determine how long it should take to send a response. In cases where your server is on a link that may be slow at times, increasing this value will ensure that valid connections are not closed.

❑ **HeaderWaitTimeout**
It specifies the number of seconds the server should wait for all HTTP headers to be received before disconnecting the client. This aids in avoiding a common denial-of-service attack that attempts to create the maximum number of open connections.

Note that increasing any timeout values can be dangerous, as it can open up your server to denial-of-service attacks by allowing abnormally long requests to sit idle, thereby consuming resources.

The `ConnectionTimeout` property can be set for a web site using the property pages. The following screen can be obtained using the same manner as described previously, and clicking on the Web Site tab:

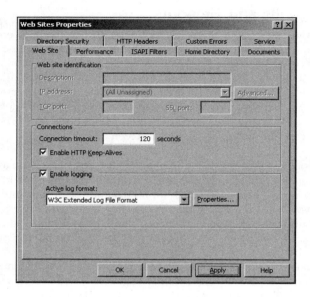

Connection timeout may be changed on the Web Site properties panel as seen in the previous screen.

Application Pool Queue Length Limits

Application pool queue length limits are used to prevent too many requests from being queued and overwhelming the server. If a new request would exceed the queue length limit, the request is rejected by sending a 503 error response and closing the connection. In cases where a single web site becomes so busy with requests that other sites on the server are suffering, an administrator might consider lowering the queue length limit for the application that serves the requests for that site. This is to constrain the number of requests that the server will queue, thereby freeing resources for other sites.

HTTP.sys sets the queue length limit to a default of 3000. IIS 6.0 resets this value to 1000 as the default. In cases where this limit is reached, an administrator might be advised to first evaluate what applications are running such that they are unable to serve requests fast enough and therefore the queue grows past 1000 requests. If the machine's CPU is not at its maximum load, **Web Gardens** are a possible solution, especially when an application is causing a queue to back up due to request processing taking an abnormally long amount of time (perhaps doing a very complex database operation). In cases where the CPU is at its maximum load, and the application cannot be further optimized, it might be time to invest in more server hardware.

Logging

Text-based logging of HTTP requests is now handled by HTTP.sys, bringing performance and reliability gains to IIS 6.0. Because this logging is done at the kernel level, the worker processes need not worry about concurrency issues when writing to log files. However, the ODBC and custom logging modules are still handled by the worker processes. These methods often (especially in the case of ODBC) rely upon a database (such as Microsoft SQL Server) that handles concurrency issues; therefore, worker processes should not be impacted.

! **If custom log modules or ODBC logging is used, kernel mode caching will be automatically disabled by IIS. This is done specifically to prevent the log from missing hits that are retrieved from the cache.**

Logging Mode (file format)	Process
W3C Extended (as defined by the World Wide Web Consortium's Working Draft *WD-logfile-960323*, found at http://www.w3.org/pub/WWW/TR/WD-logfile.html)	HTTP.sys
IIS	HTTP.sys
NCSA	HTTP.sys
Centralized Binary Logging	HTTP.sys
ODBC	w3wp.exe
Custom	w3wp.exe

For more detailed information about logging, see *Chapter 6.*

The Web Administration Service

The **Web Administration Service (WAS)**, also known as the process manager, is a user mode component of W3SVC, responsible for process management and configuration. WAS works with the metabase to handle the configuration information passed to HTTP.sys and is used in the management of worker processes. WAS is also responsible for starting and managing the operation of worker processes, including monitoring the health of worker processes. We refer to the Web Administration Service as WAS as well as the process manager.

When IIS is first started, the WAS swings into action. It reads the configuration information from the metabase file, and initializes the namespace routing tables in HTTP.sys. Basically, it means that an entry is made for each application. This entry will help HTTP.sys to decide which application pool to forward the request, depending on the URLs mapped to the application pool. HTTP.sys uses this information to set up request queues for the application pools. All these steps are completed before HTTP.sys starts accepting requests.

When new applications and application pools are added, WAS configures HTTP.sys accordingly. This involves configuring HTTP.sys to accept requests for new URLs, setting up new request queues, and indicating which application pool to forward the requests for new URLs. WAS manages the lifetime of worker processes. That entails starting worker processes, monitoring their health, and restarting them as and when necessary.

Application Pools

One of the key features of IIS 6.0 is Application Pools. Application pools define a set of one or more web applications served by one or more worker processes. Application pools allow different web applications to be separated such that they can be served by separate worker processes in separate application pools. Web applications can also be grouped into an application pool in order to share configuration settings. Each application pool is a separate Windows process (an instance of w3wp.exe), and is completely independent of other application pools, having no facilities for communicating between each other. Each application pool represents a request queue within HTTP.sys. They are considered completely segregated process spaces by design. Application pools can serve a single web application (such as an ISAPI application or ASP.NET page) or multiple applications. Multiple web sites may be placed in a single application pool, and any web directory or virtual directory can be assigned to an application pool.

The application and application pool for a web site can be configured by using the property pages for the web site. Clicking the Home Directory tab on the property pages displays the settings:

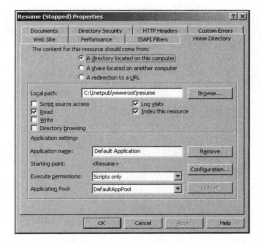

Application pools allow configuration settings to be specified independently from other groups of web applications. You can specify the health monitoring aspects of each application pool, and schedule application pool recycling based on the number of hits, and the amount of memory used, or uptime. Each application pool can be configured to conserve resources by stopping its worker process after a configurable amount of idle time, and limit the size of its request queue.

When IIS 6.0 is installed, one application pool is created as the default application pool for all sites. In the following screenshot, you will see that all of the web sites are running under the single default application pool; DefaultAppPool.

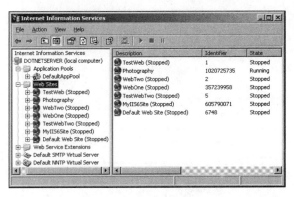

If you are hosting a single site, you should consider using this default application pool, though you may find it useful to rename it to something more meaningful, related to your application. If, on the other hand, you are hosting multiple web sites on a single server, you could create separate application pools for each site; thereby isolating them from interfering with each other, and allowing you to maintain stricter security control by configuring the worker processes to have different privileges.

In the previous example, if we wanted to isolate our Photography site, perhaps because we wanted more control over the applications within the site, we could create a new application pool and place the site within it.

In the previous figure, right-click on the Application Pools, then click New | Application Pool to bring up the Add New Application Pool panel:

Creating a new application pool is as simple as providing it with a name, and giving it either default settings (which you can customize later), or copying the settings of an existing application pool.

Selecting the application pool for your application is as simple as choosing an available application pool from the drop-down box located in the Home Directory tab of your application's properties:

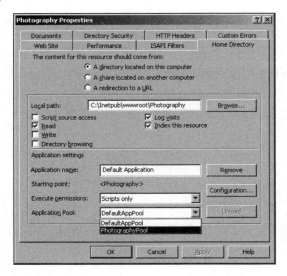

In this scenario, the Photography web site was put into its own application pool, isolating it from other applications. In a real-world scenario, this could be done because there might be a large number of sizable images being displayed. Hence, finer control over configuration will be desired, as well as a higher degree of isolation for image processing applications.

Another possible scenario in which application pools are useful is where you have both a staging and a production version of the same site. You might consider using different application pools to provide more separation (and possibly different configurations) between the production and testing versions.

Separating applications into independent processes eases a number of management tasks, such as bringing a site online or offline, making changes, managing resources, or debugging. This is definitely an advantage over previous versions. Much like the architecture of IIS 5 out-of-process applications (like ISAPI applications), separation is determined by URI namespace. As described before, HTTP.sys routes requests to a particular application pool based on a combination of either web site name or IP address, port, and URL prefix.

Application Pool Identity

The identity of an application pool is the **user account** under which the worker process runs.

You can assign a pre-defined account or a user-configurable account to an application pool as its identity. Changing the identity is accomplished from the application pool properties page; accessible by right-clicking on the application pool you wish to change:

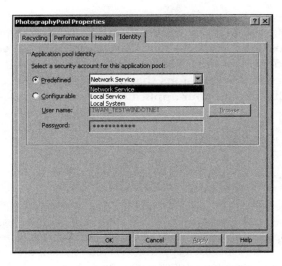

The identity is configurable via an application pool property, represented in the metabase as /LM/W3SVC/AppPools/<AppPoolID>/AppPoolIdentity, and contains the following possible values:

Property Value	Description
0	**LocalSystem Account**. Member of the IIS_WPG group. The IIS_WPG group is a user group installed by IIS 6.0 that provides the minimum set of privileges required by IIS. This group provides a convenient way to use a specific user for the identity account without having to manually assign the proper privileges to that account. If the configured account you create is not in the IIS_WPG group and does not have the appropriate permissions, the worker process will not start, and an error will be logged to the system event log.
1	**LocalService Account**. Member of IIS_WPG group. Unlike NetworkService (below), the LocalService account has no network privileges, and should be used if the web application has no need for access outside the server upon which it is hosted.
2 (default)	**NetworkService Account**. Member of IIS_WPG group. This is the lowest privileged account of the three pre-defined accounts.
3	**Configured Account**. Set the property WAMUserName and WAMUserPass to the name and password of the account to use.

> **It is always good practice, when choosing an identity, to select the least possible privileges necessary to accomplish your goals. An identity with privileges like LocalSystem will give your application permissions that might constitute security vulnerability, should your application be compromised.**

See also the discussion on impersonation in *Chapter 7*.

Demand Start of Application Pools

When the first request for a URL arrives, and if it is a part of the namespace for an application pool, the worker process (or first worker process in the case of a Web Garden) for that application pool is started. This feature, known as **Demand Start**, ensures that processes for little–used applications aren't started, even when there are no requests, and would consume resources by sitting idle.

The process manager reads the configuration information for application pools at startup time. The configuration manager initializes the namespace routing table within HTTP.sys, with one entry for each application pool. These entries comprise the regions of URI namespace for each application pool and the maximum number of worker processes for the group (typically only one, but more than one in the case of Web Gardens). This initialization configures HTTP.sys to recognize that there is an application pool available to respond to requests in a particular part of the namespace. When a request comes into HTTP.sys for an application pool and there are no processes available to handle it, HTTP.sys notifies the process manager, which starts the worker process. In the interim, HTTP.sys queues the request (and any further requests) until the process is ready.

Application Health Monitoring

Nobody writes perfect software. Even the best applications have bugs. IIS 6.0 helps manage this inevitability by constantly monitoring the health of applications and taking both preventive, as well as corrective, measures. IIS 6.0 can help diagnose problems such as memory leaks over time and access violations, and help take appropriate actions to deal with them. WAS will consider an application "unhealthy" if it has crashed, hung or terminated abnormally. All of the available IIS threads in the worker process are blocked, or the application notifies IIS directly that a problem exists.

Health Detection

You can configure an application pool to periodically "ping" a worker process, and take action if a response is not received. **Pinging** is accomplished via a named pipe between WAS and the worker process. A message is sent between WAS and the worker process over the named pipe. If the ping succeeds (the message is received and a response is sent), WAS will presume that the worker process is in good health. If there is a problem, like the worker process not responding in time, WAS can either restart the worker process or execute user-defined actions. Worker processes implement pinging in their own thread pool, so you need not implement any special code in your applications to benefit from this feature. The PingingEnabled metabase property controls whether an application pool will implement pinging, and the PingInterval property configures the number of seconds between successive checks.

Normal operation of an application

When a worker process is performing normally, it sends ReceiveRequest message to HTTP.sys. Once HTTP.sys receives a request, it will try to complete a ReceiveRequest call from the worker process. If there are no such calls pending, the new request is queued in HTTP.sys, up to the queue limit.

When an application crashes

When a worker process crashes (and exits), any `ReceiveRequests` which have completed to the worker process, will have their respective connections reset. The client will see TCP resets (`Winsock 10054` errors). Any requests that are on the `HTTP.sys` queue are not negatively affected by a worker process crash, since they aren't associated with a worker process yet. When the process fails, the process manager will detect the crash and can restart the process, which will then process the requests on the queue.

> **This changes if a debugger (such as Visual Studio) is attached to the worker process. In this case, the debugger catches the crash. Since the process is still active, the client will see a hung connection and will eventually timeout. For details on how to attach a worker process to a debugger, refer to *Chapter 7*.**

Rapid Fail

In the event an application pool experiences a certain number of crashes in a certain amount of time, the pool may be completely shutdown. The number of crashes and the amount of time after which the pool is shut down can be configured for each pool. Additionally, you can manually put an application pool into a **Rapid Fail** state. When this state is entered, `HTTP.sys` will return a 503 Service Unavailable message to any requests for the shutdown application pool. This state reduces the processing overhead on the server, as requests for failed applications never make it out of kernel mode.

You can configure the properties related to the health of applications in a pool using the property pages of the application pool. Right-click on any application pool entry in the IIS Manager and select the Health tab:

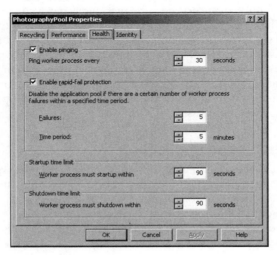

Orphan Worker Processes and Debugging

If a worker process does not respond to a ping, the process still exists even though it is seen to be in a locked state. You can configure IIS to start an application or a script in this case. Additionally, if applications have the debugging action enabled, a new worker process will be started, and the misbehaving worker process will remain available for debugging. In other words, the worker processes will not be terminated by WAS, enabling you to attach a debugger for further evaluation.

! **Leaving a large number of locked worker processes around without shutting them down can quickly eat up resources. If you enable debugging, make sure that you actually debug and then shut down the misbehaving process.**

Applications declaring "Unhealthy"

ISAPI applications may directly report themselves as "unhealthy", so that they are recycled, via the new server support function HSE_REQ_REPORT_UNHEALTHY. To use this function, the application pool containing your ISAPI application must have pinging enabled, as it is during the ping that the unhealthy state is checked.

This is how ASP and ASP.NET recycle themselves. If the ASP ISAPI extension detects that too many of its threads are blocking, it will use this function to signal a recycle.

! **Signaling that your ISAPI application is unhealthy and should be recycled will recycle the worker process for the application pool containing your ISAPI application. If there are other applications in the application pool served by that worker process, they will be affected.**

Application Recycling

IIS can restart (refresh) worker processes within an application pool on a scheduled basis. This is especially useful in cases where you're running web applications that are both poorly behaved and cannot be modified. Recycling can be configured for elapsed time, number of requests served, specific times, memory usage, or on demand. Recycling happens in one of two possible ways; either the worker processes can be stopped and a new one started, or worker processes can be recycled in an "overlapping" fashion.

The first option is straightforward; worker processes are stopped when a certain condition that has been configured is satisfied for example, after the process services a certain number of requests. In an **overlapping recycle**, the running process is allowed to complete processing the remaining requests in its queue while a new process is created. Because HTTP.sys is responsible for queuing requests to application pools, a recycled worker process will have new requests held by HTTP.sys until it is ready to accept them, providing uninterrupted service. After the new worker process starts and is ready to accept traffic, new requests (as well as queued ones from the intervening time) are routed to the new worker process, while the old process finishes and shuts down gracefully. This provides uninterrupted service by allowing the old process to complete (or "drain") existing requests before it shuts down. If the old process takes too long (in the case where it has crashed and is hanging), IIS will shut it down forcibly.

! **Since the timeout value of an overlapping recycle (and for that matter, any shutdown condition) is configurable, it is possible to forcefully shut down the old process before it has finished servicing existing requests.**

The following table outlines the different methods of process recycling. Note that these options are not mutually exclusive and you can use one or more of them at the same time. Remember, as far as possible, you should attempt to fix the problem at the source (your application) rather than rely on recycling.

Recycle Mode	Description
Elapsed Time	Recycles worker processes after an elapsed number of minutes. Use this mode if you know that your applications are failing after a certain time period.
Number of Requests	Recycles worker processes after a specific number of HTTP requests. Use this mode if you know that your applications are failing after a certain number of requests.
Scheduled Time(s)	Recycles worker processes at specified times within a 24-hour period.
Memory Usage	Recycles worker processes based on the amount of virtual memory used by the w3wp.exe process. Use this mode if you know that your application has a memory leak.
On Demand	Recycles worker processes when an IIS administrator instructs IIS to do so. Use this mode to recycle a particular application rather than restart the entire web service.

! **When an application is recycled, you will almost surely lose any session state that you had stored, unless you have persisted it elsewhere (such as to a database).**

You can set an application to be recycled by configuring the settings accessed through the properties page of an application as described for the previous screen and clicking on the Recycling tab:

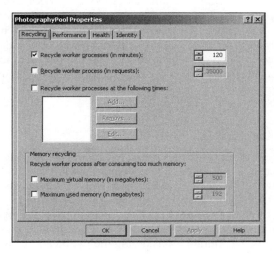

Idle Process Timeout

An application pool can be configured to shut down worker processes that have sat idle for a configurable amount of time, thereby freeing up resources. New worker processes will be demand started when new requests are received for their application pool. The settings for timeouts can be accessed by opening the property pages for an application pool and clicking the Performance tab:

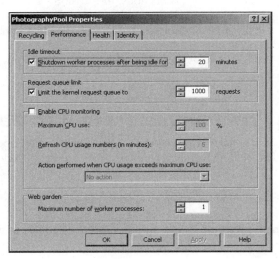

Web Gardens

An application pool may configure the amount of worker processes assigned to the pool. A **Web Garden** is created when multiple worker processes exist within a single application pool. Do not confuse Web Garden with Web Farm, which is a term used to describe multiple physical servers, all hosting the same web application (usually for load-balancing purposes). Web gardens improve both the performance and reliability of a web application. Web gardens can provide additional available worker processes, when one or more are heavily loaded or locked in the process of servicing a request.

Using Web Gardens

To make the best use of Web Gardens for process balancing, multiple application request queues are created and HTTP.sys is responsible for distributing the load across the processes in a Web Garden. HTTP.sys will route requests from different connections to the processes in a round-robin fashion. For example, if a Web Garden has three processes, the first three requests from different connections will go to the first, second, and third process in order. The fourth request will then go to the first process, and the cycle will continue. Considering the overhead involved in operations that are serialized for locking, this method provides performance advantages.

Session State in Web Gardens

Remember that HTTP is a stateless protocol. What that means is that if a connection is closed after processing a request, there is no guarantee that the same worker process will service future requests, even from the same client. In cases where session state must be maintained across different connections, the session state could be lost if a subsequent request were sent to a different worker process. While keeping the connection open is one possible solution, it is recommended that state be persisted to ensure that it is available. What this means is storing the state in an external location such as a database – for example, ASP.NET provides the ability to store session state in a SQL Server database.

Application Pool Parameters in Web Gardens

While most settings for application pools remain unchanged when operating a Web Garden, there are a few settings which have modified meanings. They are:

- ❑ **MaxProcesses**
  This is the property to change to create a Web Garden. By default, all application pools have one process and MaxProcesses is set to "1". Increasing the value of MaxProcesses to the number of worker process instances, you will create a Web Garden for your application pool.

❏ **IdleTimeout**
It is individually calculated on a per-process basis, allowing processes to timeout individually.

❏ **PeriodicRestartTime**
It states that all of the processes in a Web Garden will recycle within the time specified. For example, if a Web Garden consists of four processes and `PeriodicRestartTime` is set to 16 hours, each process will be recycled every four hours. It should be apparent that this distribution of restart times maintains that each process is recycled every `PeriodicRestartTime` hours. In the event of a restart due to a crash or other problem, that time period is reset to when the process is restarted.

❏ **PeriodicRestartRequests**
It operates in a similar fashion to `PeriodicRestartTime`. For example, in a Web Garden with four processes and a `PeriodicRestartRequests` value of 80,000 requests, the first process will recycle after 20,000, the second after 40,000, the third after 60,000, and the fourth after 80,000 requests. Each worker process will then recycle every 80,000 requests in this manner.

❏ **RapidFailProtection**
It calculates the total number of failures across all processes in the Web Garden when comparing them to the time interval (`RapidFailProtectionMaxCrashes` over `RapidFailProtectionInterval`).

Processor Affinity

Processor affinity is an application pool property that forces worker processes to run on specific processors on a multi-processor machine. A Web Garden provides its best performance gains on a multi-processor server, where each worker process in a Web Garden may be assigned to run on a separate processor. For example, on a server that has eight processors, an application pool might be configured to run on four of those processors.

`SMPProcessorAffinityMask` is the mask for all processes running in a Web Garden. To set processor affinity, you must set the `SMPAffinitized` property to true, and then set the `SMPProcessorAffinityMask` to the range of CPUs you wish your worker processes to be bound. In the previous example, the affinity mask would be set for the processors numbered zero through three, and all worker processes in the application pool would run on the first four processors.

Summary

With the new kernel mode driver, HTTP.sys, and the new worker process isolation mode, IIS 6.0 is a platform that extends the capabilities as well as the performance and reliability of the web application platform. The new capabilities of IIS 6.0 allow for the offering of new services based on the web server, and the performance enhancements allow for more services to be offered on existing hardware, while simultaneously improving the reliability of those new as well as existing services. Coupled with an enhanced ability to maintain and configure these new features, the new request architecture of IIS 6.0 is clearly a step forward.

In this chapter, we looked at the new request architecture of IIS 6.0, which provides many improvements over the previous versions. IIS 6.0 separates the request processing code and the application handling code into HTTP.sys and Web Administration Service respectively. HTTP.sys is a kernel mode driver and provides facilities of kernel level request queues, response caching, logging, and configuring the quality of service provided to the clients. WAS uses the metabase settings to configure the request queues for HTTP.sys. It also provides the facility of creating and monitoring worker processes for applications to run.

IIS 6.0 provides a new Worker Process Isolation Mode, in addition to the IIS 5 Isolation Mode. The new mode entails more features, such as application isolation, multiple application pools, application health monitoring, rapid fail protection, and application recycling. Configuring an application pool as a Web Garden and using the processor affinity feature can improve the performance of the applications. IIS also provides the option of running applications in the IIS 5 isolation mode for backward compatibility in situations that require it. We saw how to choose between these two options and to switch between them.

To summarize, here are some of the features and components of the new request architecture:

- Kernel-mode HTTP listener (HTTP.sys)
- Web Administration Service (WAS)
- Application Pools
- Worker Process Isolation Mode
- Web Gardens
- Health Monitoring and Rapid Fail Detection
- Recycling
- Idle Timeout

In the next chapter, we will take a comprehensive look at the security aspects of IIS 6.0.

IIS 6

Programming

Handbook

3

3

Security in IIS 6.0

Unquestionably, one of the most drastic improvements in IIS 6.0 is in the realm of security. Microsoft has taken a proactive stance towards security by adopting a policy of "lockdown" on most aspects of IIS 6.0. Indeed, IIS 6.0 is not installed by default along with Windows Server 2003. This is to prevent scenarios like those in the past, where many administrators would leave IIS in a default configuration when installing a new server; often not realizing that IIS had been installed at all. In its previous default configuration, IIS had all services enabled, including those that were not needed, and often left unsecured as well. Furthermore, many administrators neglected to apply critical security patches to IIS, as they were under the impression that their database server, for example, was not running IIS in the first place.

When IIS 6.0 is installed, only static content is enabled by default. All dynamic content including CGI, ASP, ASP.NET, and ISAPI are prohibited until specifically enabled. When IIS 6.0 is installed as an upgrade, this content is also disabled, requiring an administrator to re-enable those content types that are needed.

Security in IIS 6.0 is more than just disabling and enabling features and capabilities, and covers a number of different realms. When taken as a whole, IIS 6.0 security features help provide for a more secure server. Controlling access to your server, determining who can view certain pages and who can run certain web applications are all vital components of a robust security solution provided by IIS. IIS 6.0 allows you to control the security picture at different levels, from a whole-server standpoint all the way down to individual files.

We will take a look at how this is all achieved by considering the following aspects of security:

❏   Extension Management

❏   Web site and FTP site Authentication

❏   Access Control

❏   Cryptography

❏   Application Pool/ Worker Process identities

❏   Timeouts and Limits

Before we go into the details, let's take a brief overview of the security process.

An Overview of the Security Process

The first steps in securing an installation of IIS 6.0 are broad actions taken to reduce the attack surface of the web server itself, and then putting in place the configuration necessary to authenticate (identify) and authorize (grant permission) the users of your server. These steps, while simple and intuitive, form the backbone for a secure web server:

❏   Install only what is needed

❏   Authenticate Clients

❏   Authorize Clients

Install Only What Is Needed

When setting up IIS 6.0, it is always best to install and enable only those services that you need, for example, some ISAPI extensions or ASP.NET, and set up user accounts and groups with minimal permissions necessary to accomplish the tasks. If you do not need any functionality, such as CGI, leave it disabled.

Although IIS 6.0 has many new features to reduce the vulnerability of a web server to attacks; remember that the weakest link is often the administrator who wrongly configures a server, leaving a security hole open for an attacker to exploit.

Authenticating Clients

Before a request for a web page, web application, or FTP site is returned, IIS 6.0 performs a number of security permission and authorization checks. The request is then processed only if all of these checks succeed. However, before authorization checks are run, the client must be authenticated. When a request is received, IIS 6.0 will first check if the IP address from which the request was sent is allowed to make such a request. If that succeeds, the identity under which the request is being processed is evaluated. In other words, the web server must verify that the identity of the client is known (or satisfied that the client is "anonymous", which as we will see later, is a valid identity itself).

There are different options available that decide what type of users will be allowed access to the enabled services. You must carefully choose these options so that only the right kind of users, with proper credentials are allowed access to these services.

Authorizing Clients

To perform operations like file read, write, or execute, as part of providing the services, the server makes use of web server accounts. These accounts are built into IIS 6.0 and set to varying level of privileges. The identity of the client is mapped to these accounts. Thus, the client can request operations that his account allows.

Based upon the identity of the client, IIS determines if the permissions for the user account permit the request. Finally, the actual file permissions under **NT File System** (**NTFS**) are checked against the identity of the client. These checks are applied to every request and determine what happens to the request. If any of the security checks fail, the client will most likely see a 403 Access Forbidden or 401 Access is denied error returned.

The following diagram outlines the procedure of authentication and authorization in IIS 6.0:

Figure 1

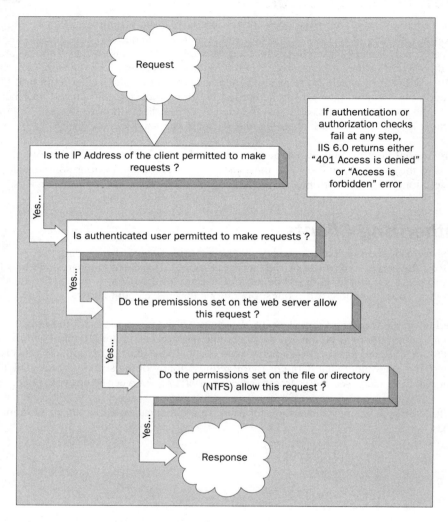

Now that we've outlined the steps, let's take a closer look at how they actually work and how they can be configured.

Extension Management

As we've seen, when IIS 6.0 is installed, only static content (`.htm`, `.bmp`, `.jpg`, and the like) is enabled by default. Additional services, such as ASP, ASP.NET, CGI, Server-Side Includes, WebDAV Publishing, and ISAPI extensions and filters need to be explicitly enabled by administrators. Requests for these types of content will receive a 404 Not Found error, as if they did not exist on the server, unless they are enabled. This new attitude towards extension management ("locked down" policy) will be the first thing an IIS 6.0 administrator notices, and the first task to carry out to enable the new server.

To configure your server properly, two tasks must be undertaken. First, you must configure which web service extensions will be allowed, as they are all disallowed by default. Second, you can define any additional web service extensions and the programs that will handle requests for those extensions.

Disabling Unknown and Unneeded Extensions

IIS 6.0 now requires the explicit enabling of web service extensions. In the following example, all extensions are allowed, with the exception of unknown CGI extensions. The following screen can be accessed by starting the **IIS Manager** (Go to Start | Programs | Administrative tools | Internet Information Services. Alternatively, you can enter inetmgr in the Run window):

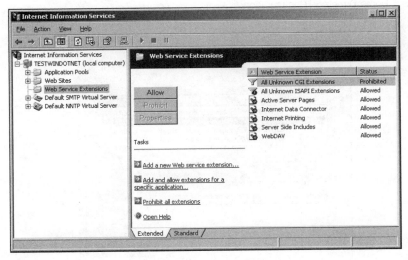

For each service extension, the Allow and Prohibit tabs can be used to enable and disable the specific extension. For example, if in your application, you do not make use of Active Server Pages (ASP), it is recommended that you prohibit the ASP web service extension. Ask yourself, why enable a feature that is unused, and increase the potential attack surface for a malicious user?

Enabling New Extensions

In addition to enabling a web service extension, you will also want to ensure that the filename extension relating to the technology is enabled as well; otherwise the file will be treated as plain HTML and not routed to the appropriate executable. New filename extensions are added in the Application Configuration section of a web site's properties, and can also be added globally from the properties of the Web Sites folder.

Additionally, it is also useful to examine the list of filename extensions and their related programs, and remove mappings for programs that are no longer used.

If you mapped a particular filename extension to an executable, to protect the contents of that file, then removing the mapping will make that file readable, as it will now be treated as plain HTML. For example, if you stored passwords to a database in an ASP.NET web.config file, that file is protected from viewing by the fact that the .config filename extension is mapped to the ASP.NET program. Removing the .config mapping would make your web.config file viewable. If you remove the mapping, ensure that you also remove the file, or set permissions on it such that it is not viewable by anyone not authorized to see it.

To enable new extensions, right-click the web site name in IIS Manager. Then go to Properties | Home Directory | Configuration:

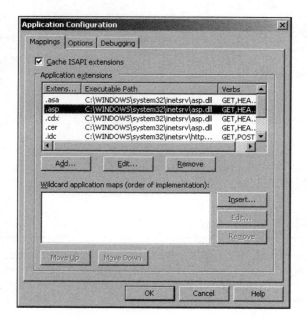

In this example, the extension .asp is set to be executed by the ASP DLL, and respond to the GET, HEAD, POST, and DEBUG verbs.

From the Application Configuration section, you can also change the executable path to be called for particular extensions.

The following dialog appears on clicking the Add tab on the Application Configuration window shown in the previous diagram:

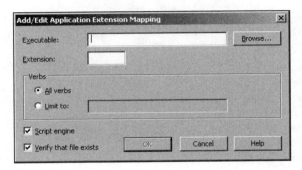

Adding a new extension consists of selecting the executable to handle requests for the extension, and selecting the verbs that will receive responses.

Web Site Authentication

IIS 6.0 provides a number of different ways to control access to your web sites, FTP sites, and even provides the ability to control access down to the individual file level. The first step in the process is **Authentication**, which is the act of determining the identity of the individual (or computer) requesting access to your web site. Based upon the results of authentication, the appropriate permission sets can be applied, leading to a decision as to whether to serve the file or not.

There are several authentication methods available for web sites and FTP sites. These can be set by right-clicking the appropriate web or FTP site in the IIS Manager and selecting the Directory Security tab. That brings up the authentication and access control frame, which contains the Edit tab. Clicking on the Edit tab will bring up the following window, which lets you select the desirable authentication method:

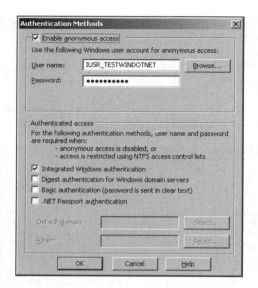

Now let's look at the different authentication options available in more detail.

Anonymous

Most public web sites need to allow **Anonymous Authentication**, which is used to grant access to web sites that require no authentication for security. Anonymous authentication causes the web site to allow access via the anonymous user account (IUSR_MACHINENAME, which we will see a little later in the chapter). This account should be configured to have the least possible privileges needed to properly serve the web site's needs, such as read permission on all necessary files, but not others, and execute permission only for scripts necessary to the site.

It is important to note that if you enable anonymous authentication, IIS will attempt to use it first, even if you have other authentication methods enabled. In cases where you have content that you wish to protect, ensure that the anonymous account does not have permission to access that content, in which case further authentication methods (provided they have been enabled) will be tried.

Basic

Basic Authentication uses an account name and password, sent in clear non-encrypted base64 encoded text. Since the information is sent in the clear, it is possible for an attacker to monitor network traffic and intercept account names and passwords with relative ease. Basic authentication is often combined with **Secure Sockets Layer** (**SSL**) to ensure that the passwords aren't intercepted.

You can select the domain for this authentication method by accessing the Authentication Methods pane as described previously, and clicking on the checkbox for Basic authentication. That will enable the buttons for selecting Default domain and Realm:

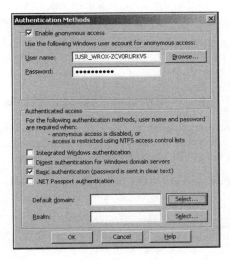

You can select the default domain for your users by clicking on the appropriate Select button:

Digest and Advanced Digest

Digest and **Advanced Digest Authentication** send the account name and password as a hashed message digest. This digest (or **MD5** hash) ensures that the account and password cannot be determined from the digest itself. Digest authentication requires the user to be a member of (or trusted by) the same domain as the server and have a valid account on the domain controller. Hence, this mode is not ideal for general Internet use.

When a request for a file is received by IIS, the server returns a message to the client indicating that Digest Authentication is being used, which also includes the realm name for the authentication. This prompts the user for a name and password pair, which is encoded into an MD5 digest and returned to the server. IIS then sends the hash to the domain controller for authentication before serving the file (if the authentication succeeds).

In IIS 6.0, the preferred mode is Advanced Digest due to its higher level of security in storing user credentials. The Digest and Advanced Digest modes are identical, except that Advanced Digest protects the local copy of the user credentials better by storing them in the domain controller as an MD5 hash, as opposed to clear-text. Since they are stored in digest form, they cannot be discovered, even by those with access to the active directory.

Like Basic authentication, using Digest and Advanced Digest combined with SSL provides for much better security. It should also be noted that both Digest and Advanced Digest modes require Internet Explorer version 5 or later.

You can set this authentication method by accessing the Authentication Methods pane as described previously and selecting the Digest authentication checkbox:

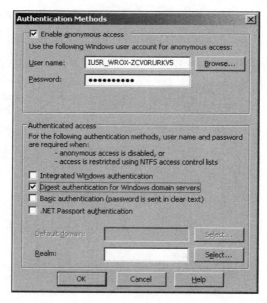

You can select the realm for your users by clicking the Select button, which brings up the Browse for domain pane, similar to the one given previously for basic authentication.

Integrated

Integrated Windows Authentication, the default authentication mode for Windows Server 2003, sends the username and password as a hashed value or a **Kerberos** ticket when Kerberos is used. Formerly known as **NTLM**, this mode is most often used on a company intranet, where users are expected to log in with the appropriate credentials. In this case, the users will not need to send their authentication information through an HTTP proxy, which can be problematic for this mode. Naturally, Integrated Authentication requires that clients are running on a Microsoft client on the network.

Kerberos

Kerberos Authentication uses secret key cryptography to exchange authentication information between client and server. Developed at the Massachusetts Institute of Technology, Kerberos authenticates users by encrypting a series of messages between the client and the server that are exchanged to establish the identity of the client and/or the server. For more information on Kerberos, go to http://web.mit.edu/kerberos/www/.

Client Certificate

Client Certificate Authentication uses an SSL certificate to provide authentication to IIS. While SSL uses a **server certificate** to authenticate your web site to clients, certificate authentication uses a **client certificate** to authenticate clients. This mode is most often used to provide higher security for Internet commerce applications, such as the exchange of business-to-business information like product orders, or funds transfer information, that require the secure identity of a client.

Client certificates are mapped to Windows user accounts, which then provide security permissions for your web site. You can map a single client certificate to a single user account, or many client certificates to a single user account, depending upon your needs. However, you must take into account the time-overhead in managing client certificates, especially in cases where you must maintain many of them across many machines.

You can add client certificates in the following manner. In the IIS Manager, open the appropriate web site properties window, and select the Directory Security tab. In the Secure Communications frame, click the Edit button. That will bring up the Secure Communications dialog box. Selecting Enable Client certificate mapping checkbox will enable the Edit button. Clicking on that button will bring up the following window:

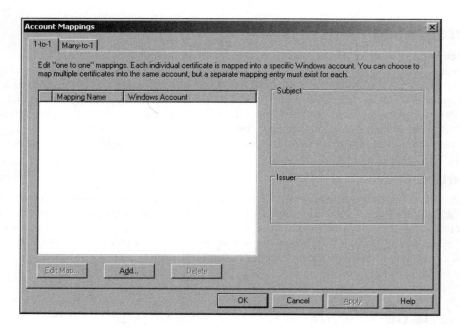

You can now add client certificates by clicking the **Add** button, and choose the mapping scheme for the certificates from the previous screen shown.

.NET Passport

.NET Passport Authentication is new to IIS 6.0, and uses an encrypted password over SSL to authenticate the client. The .NET Passport is a Microsoft service that offers a single point of sign-in across a large number of "Passport enabled" web sites, authentication, and other services. Passport is part of Microsoft's **.NET Framework**, and allows you to map Passport Authentication information to local authentication upon which to base your authorization decisions. Passport uses an internal mix of SSL and cookies, and redirects to enable a secure sign-in from a central Passport server.

An important concept to remember is that Passport does not itself authorize permissions for a user. It merely authenticates the user and presents your site with verification of that authentication. In fact, your web site will never see the authenticated user's password. Instead, Passport will provide you with an authentication cookie comprised of a pair of encrypted timestamps that represent when the user logged in.

When selecting which authentication modes your site will support, remember that your site is only as secure as the *least secure* mode you offer. In other words, even if you offer client certificate authentication, if you are offering basic authentication, it may be used as well.

FTP Site Authentication

FTP sites use one of two possible authentication modes. They are:

❑ **Anonymous FTP Authentication**
It does not require the client to submit any credentials. Users log in with the account name "anonymous" and are prompted to enter their e-mail address as the password. The password is ignored, however, and anonymous access is always granted when this mode is enabled. Like anonymous web access, all requests are handled under the IUSR_MACHINE account, which has the minimum level of privileges necessary.

❑ **Basic FTP Authentication**
It requires a user name and password, but sends both in clear, unencrypted text, which allows for interception by anyone monitoring network traffic. To ensure that users cannot send their information over an unencrypted link, an option to allow *only* anonymous access is available.

If you are going to allow your users to use FTP to transfer files, ensure that any file-level protection you need is enabled by setting the appropriate permissions on the files and directories that your users will access. Create a directory for each user and set the permissions such that only that user (or a group to which the user belongs) has the appropriate access permissions. This will ensure that an anonymous user cannot access files and directories that they should not.

You can set the authentication mode for an FTP site by accessing its property pages in the IIS Manager window and selecting Security Accounts tab:

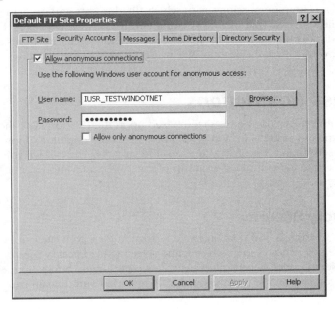

Delegated Authentication

In addition to being concerned with the authentication of clients who access your web server, you might also be concerned with the authentication of your web applications across your network. "Delegation" is the term used to describe the granting of authentication rights to your web applications that access the server and network resources to perform their functions. In other words, an application may be delegated the same rights as a user or service other than itself, to access information on other networked servers. Windows Server 2003 adds the "Constrained, Delegated Authorization" feature, which IIS uses to accomplish this task.

This new functionality entails some warnings. Specifically, you should ensure that any delegated authorization you grant is for specific services, and not a blanket authorization for every service. Furthermore, any delegation you create should not require the credentials of the client to be passed to other servers. While you may want to allow clients to access resources, you may not have control over those resources or their administrators, and passing the client's authentication information might allow it to be compromised.

Access Control

After authentication, the next step is authorization of client. Where authentication dealt with the question of "who goes there", authorization deals with the "are you allowed in here?" aspect of security.

IIS 6.0 allows for setting permissions as to which IP addresses and domain names be allowed or denied access. That includes setting permissions for web sites, FTP sites, as well as virtual directories. Permissions may be set on individual directories and files, as well as by URL with URL authorization. We will now look at these settings in detail.

IP Address Restrictions

FTP and web site access may be restricted based upon the IP address of the client. Like all other IP-restriction systems in Windows, you can set the default to allow access or deny access based upon a list of IP addresses and subnets. This allows you to grant or deny access to a specific computer or group of computers in a subnet. For IIS 6.0, only IPv4 is supported.

Web Directory Security

The settings for IP address and domain name restriction for a web site can be modified by accessing the properties of the web site, and selecting the Directory Security tab. Then selecting the Edit tab under Authentication and access control frame brings up the following window. Now you can set the permissions for IP addresses and domain names:

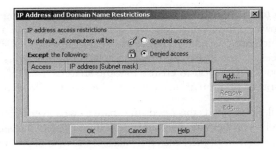

FTP Directory Security

The settings for FTP directory security are similar to those of web sites and can be accessed in a similar fashion. The following screenshot gives the settings for the default FTP site and can be accessed by clicking the Directory Security tab in the FTP properties window.

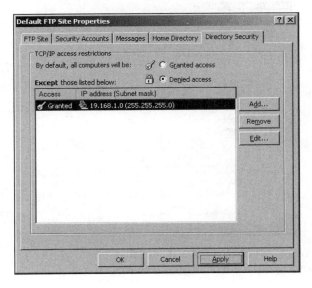

Virtual Directory Security

Virtual directories are not actual directories, but are "aliases" for physical directories upon which you can assign an easier name (for example, /pictures instead of C:\sites\photography\latest\pictures). Virtual directories are useful both for their ability to make the naming easier as well as for the fact that they can be mapped to any local or network directory. Virtual directories can be secured using local user authentication. What is new to IIS 6.0 is the ability to delegate authentication of virtual directories, mapped to **Universal Naming Convention** (**UNC**) paths, to local authentication.

In the **Virtual Directory Creation Wizard** (available by right-clicking on a web site, and then selecting New and then Virtual Directory) we can either use the authenticated user's credentials, which are passed through to the share; or specify a specific user name and password for access to the share. Both methods have their benefits and drawbacks. Using a specific account allows you to ensure that the share is available. You might use this in cases where you want anonymous access to the files on the share.

You want to be careful, however, as this opens the share to whatever rights the account you specify has. Alternatively, you can pass the authenticated user's credentials through to the share. This includes the IUSR_MACHINENAME credentials in the case of anonymous access. You could then set finer control over the permissions of the files and directories in the share.

In the following example, we have created a virtual directory called Virtuoso as a share located on another computer. We can set this by accessing the properties of the virtual directory and selecting the appropriate option:

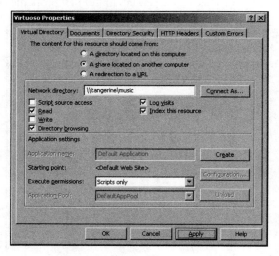

In this case, the computer tangerine has a share called music, to which we can connect. We then assign permissions for reading and directory browsing.

URL Authorization

URL Authorization allows you to set access controls based on the URL of the web application being accessed. URL Authorization is implemented through an **Authorization Manager**, which keeps an **Authorization Store**, either in the Active Directory or in an XML configuration file. This store keeps all configuration and security information for defining roles for users of your web application. Role-based security, as it is called, defines permission roles for your application, which are then assigned to authorized users.

One drawback to URL Authorization in non-intranet situations is that it requires you to create configuration information for each user who will be using your web application.

File System Permissions

NTFS allows you to set permissions on the files under your web server for finer control of permissions. Access can be granted or denied to any user or group, including the standard accounts related to IIS. For example, the anonymous user (IUSR_MACHINENAME) should have read and execute permissions for any file that you wish to allow an anonymous web client to see. For files that require an authenticated user, it is a recommended security procedure to set the NTFS permissions such that only that user has access to the file. In most cases, groups should handle access control, allowing you to add users to the group as needed.

Do not confuse NTFS permissions with web permissions, as set in the IIS Manager. Web permissions apply to anyone accessing your web site, whereas NTFS permissions apply to specific files and directories, and are set for specific users and groups. Web permissions provide broad control over an entire site or virtual directory, and NTFS permissions provide specific control over individual files and folders. Web permissions and NTFS permissions go hand in hand in providing a complete security picture.

IIS Built-In Accounts

Certain accounts are built-in to IIS (created when IIS is installed) with their own default set of permissions. The permissions are granted on both user and group boundaries. The permissions and group memberships for these built-in accounts are set at installation time.

The various IIS accounts are:

❑   **Local System**
    It has a high level of permissions, giving it full access rights to the entire system.

❑   **Network Service**
    It has less permission than Local System, yet can access the network with the local computer's credentials. Application pools are configured by default to use this account as their identity.

❑   **Local Service**
    It has access permissions limited to the local computer only. This account should be used for worker process identities, if the worker process has no need of access outside the local server.

❑   **IIS_WPG**
    This group has the minimum permissions required to run a worker process.

❑ **IUSR_COMPUTERNAME**
This is used for anonymous access to your web site.

❑ **IWAM_COMPUTERNAME**
It is used for running out-of-process web applications when operating under IIS 5 Isolation Mode.

❑ **ASP.NET**
It is used for running ASP.NET worker process when operating under IIS 5 Isolation Mode.

Cryptography

Sending information over the Internet can be risky if that information is sensitive, such as confidential company data, or credit card numbers on a shopping web site.

SSL 3.0

To protect sensitive data, **Secure Sockets Layer (SSL)** is used. SSL encrypts the information going to and from a web site, thus protecting it from eavesdroppers. IIS uses the SSL 3.0 protocol, which provides the basis for an encrypted conversation between client and server, securely identifying the web site, and optionally, when client certificates are used, the client. You can find more information on SSL 3.0 at http://wp.netscape.com/eng/ssl3/draft302.txt.

One key advantage to using SSL is that the entire communication path is secured before any other information is sent. This means that inherently unsafe authentication methods, such as Basic Authentication, can be used with confidence that the unencrypted information contained in the authorization packets cannot be read, as they are encrypted by SSL. Furthermore, SSL encrypts the contents of the data being exchanged, eliminating the need to do so before sending. This is crucial for sites that allow clients to view and work with sensitive information such as banking records, medical records, or confidential company information.

SSL is a public-key security protocol. This means that encryption is accomplished by using a public and private **key pair**. The server creates a **session key** (also known as an **encryption key**) that the client and server use to encrypt and decrypt transferred information. The strength of the encryption is measured in bits (typically 40-bit and 128-bit). The more bits used for encryption, the more difficult it is for an attacker to "crack" the code. To enable SSL on your server, you must generate a **server certificate**.

Certificates

Certificates are electronic documents that allow clients and servers to identify themselves. Servers use certificates to establish a trusted identity in the creation of an SSL link, allowing a server to identify itself to the satisfaction of a client.

To generate a server certificate, you must either use the **Microsoft Certificate Services** (refer to http://www.microsoft.com/windows2000/techinfo/howitworks/security/windows2000csoverview.asp) or acquire your certificate from a third-party certification authority, who will verify your identity information based on the level of trust you require.

As we have previously mentioned, clients also use certificates to establish a trusted identity when authenticating to a web site.

Selectable Cryptographic Service Provider

SSL provides security in exchange for a small loss of performance due to the processor-intensive job of encrypting and decrypting transmitted and received information. IIS 6.0 now allows for a selectable **cryptographic service provider** (**CSP**), allowing the use of hardware-based and other encryption solutions to handle encryption and certificate management. Each provider handles the creation of encryption keys and has the option to store them in hardware, such as smart security cards, for additional security. All CSPs implement a consistent set of **Application Programming Interfaces** (**Crypto API**), allowing you to switch between providers, without the need to change your web application code.

Microsoft provides two cryptographic service providers by default: Secure Channel encryption with both Diffie-Hellman (DH) and RSA encryption. DH provides hashing, data signing, and generating, exchanging, and exporting DH keys, while RSA provides hashing, data signing and signature verification.

Configurable Application Pool / Worker Process Identity

As discussed in *Chapter 2*, application pools may be configured to run under any account, and not just the Local System. This allows for the prevention of a number of security vulnerabilities related to running under the Local System or Network Service accounts, which have privileges that can be taken advantage of by malicious code in applications.

Consider the case of a web application with a bug that causes a buffer overflow, which is one of the most common sources of security breaches. A malicious attacker can send data to your web application knowing that the buffer will be overrun. In this case, the extra data is often written to memory in such a way as to be executed as code. If the web application is running under Local System, the attacker's code is running as Local System as well, enabling the attacker to accomplish any number of tasks, including completely taking over the machine. Microsoft introduced a service within IIS 6.0 that checks the cache buffer periodically and anytime it is close to overflow, kills the processes in question that could be causing the overflow to happen. This is one of the new ways IIS6 guards against buffer overflow.

It must be noted that even though the new .NET **Common Language Runtime (CLR)**, used predominantly in ASP.NET, protects against common security (programming) flaws such as buffer overruns, it will be quite some time until all of the existing code that is vulnerable to these problems is made completely obsolete.

An **Application Pool Identity** is the operating system user account that serves as the process identity for the worker processes within an application pool (the account under which the process runs). You can assign a pre-defined account or a user-configurable account to an application pool as its identity. Changing the identity is accomplished from the application pool Properties page, which is accessible by right-clicking on the application pool you wish to modify. Selecting the Identity tab in the properties page displays following screen:

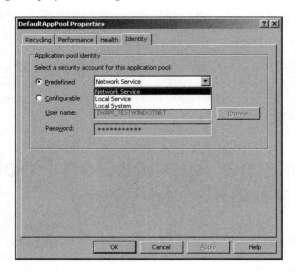

HTTP.sys Timeouts and Limits

A number of attacks, particularly **Denial-of-Service (DoS)** attacks can be mitigated by the aggressive use of timeouts and limits. **Connection Limits** control the number of simultaneous connections at any one time. The HeaderWaitTimeout property in the metabase specifies the number of seconds the server should wait for all HTTP headers to be received before disconnecting the client. This aids in avoiding a common denial-of-service attack that attempts to create the maximum number of open connections without sending a single byte of data.

Application pool queue length limits can also be used to prevent too many requests from being queued and overwhelming the server as a denial-of-service attack. If a new request would exceed the queue length limit, that request is rejected by sending a 503 error response, and closing the connection.

HTTP.sys ensures that URLs are properly decoded in a process known as **URL Canonicalization** so as to avoid attacks based upon malformed URLs and requests for system directory traversal such as ".." directories.

HTTP.sys logs all errors, including requests that cannot be routed to a worker process, or those that had an error before being routed to a worker process. This is a separate error log, which can be reviewed by administrators to identify possible attacks.

Timeouts, Connection Limits, and HTTP.sys are discussed in more detail in *Chapter 2*.

Monitoring and Maintenance

Even after you have taken care of all aspects of server security as mentioned so far in the chapter, your server can never be 100% secure all the time. New security flaws are discovered on a regular basis. As such, the most important security job once the initial configuration is complete is to stay aware of security patches, apply them as they are issued, and monitor your system.

Security Patches

Microsoft regularly issues patches to operating systems and applications, as bugs and security vulnerabilities are discovered and fixed. This includes both service packs as well as individual patches often found at the Windows Update site (http://windowsupdate.microsoft.com). If you do not run the automated patch download system, you should make it a regular part of your maintenance routine to check the appropriate Microsoft web sites to ensure that there are no unapplied patches. This is true of all server applications, not just IIS.

Monitoring Your System

In addition to ensuring that you're always running the most up-to-date patches, there are a number of logs that should be monitored for suspicious activity (at best) or evidence of security breaches (at worst).

Enabling IIS logging should be one of the first tasks you do after configuring your web site. Depending upon what kind of information you want to collect, you can select from the available formats, including a Microsoft, NCSA, W3C Extended format, or formats for sending logging information to an ODBC database or a centralized binary database. Understanding the benefits and downsides to each format is crucial to making the right decision for your site. See *Chapter 7* for more information on logging.

Another important place to monitor is the system and security log kept by Windows server. These are logs available through the Event Viewer application on your server (accessed through the Administrative tools), and will contain both housekeeping messages as well as more serious errors.

Finally, you might consider enabling file auditing, especially for changes to the files served by your web applications, and occasionally running scans on your server for potential security holes.

Summary

In this chapter, we have seen how security plays a crucial role in IIS 6.0, and how improvements to IIS have resulted in a clear and robust platform for a secure web application server.

Finally, we should put in a pitch for the Microsoft IIS Deployment Guide, which contains a wealth of information about security issues, including detailed checklists for securing your IIS server.

In this chapter, we saw how to control the security aspects of IIS 6.0 by first deciding what services to install, then authenticating the clients, and finally authorizing them. IIS 6.0 installs in a default "locked down" mode, and services other than static content have to be specifically enabled. IIS 6.0 provides various authentication methods, which ensure that only the right kind of users with proper credentials can access the web services.

We saw how to use access control features in IIS 6.0, such as IP address restrictions, URL authorizations, in-built user accounts, and NTFS permissions to enforce your security policy. We looked at a number of new features in IIS 6.0, such as support for SSL 3.0, selectable cryptographic service provider, configurable application pool identity, and connection timeouts and limits that enhance the security aspects of your server.

We will discuss the various aspects involved in administering IIS 6.0 in the next chapter.

IIS 6

Programming

Handbook

4

The XML Metabase

One of the most frustrating things in previous versions of IIS, when things went wrong, was that the data about the configuration of IIS, and the sites and applications installed in it, could become corrupted with no easy way to reinstate the system. You could make backups of information, and then fall back to that point by restoring (or overwriting) the existing (corrupted) data. However, because the data was in binary format, there was no way to manipulate the configuration data manually or see exactly why the problem had arisen.

In IIS 6.0, Microsoft has answered the user's concerns by completely changing the way that the configuration information is stored, and provided ways to manipulate this information using simple tools or through programmatic techniques. This also offers extra advantages, like making it easy to backup and restore the information, and replicate it between servers in a web farm environment.

In this chapter we will look at the way that this new configuration system works, the structure of the data, and how we can manipulate it in different ways. We'll see:

❑ What the configuration data format looks like, and how this simplifies administration

❑ How security is implemented and managed on the configuration information

❑ How we can edit this data while IIS is running

We start with an overview of the configuration data format.

Configuration Data Formats

Over the past few years, the de-facto standard for persisting data to a file or stream has evolved to use XML. Prior to this, most Windows applications and services used one of two techniques for storing configuration information. They are:

❑ Text files in the .INI file format, consisting of section and individual entries in the form:

```
[Section Name]
KeyName=Value
KeyName=Value
...etc...
```

❑ Some proprietary format, often binary in nature, which is read as a block of data and decoded into individual values by the software that uses it. This is the method used by IIS 5 and earlier versions, and is referred to as the **IIS Metabase**.

Both techniques work well, and each has its advantages and disadvantages. Using human-readable text, as in the INI file format, means that corrupted files can often be rebuilt or repaired without special tools, and without requiring the application that uses the file. However, they are more verbose, requiring extra processing by the application and using marginally more resources. There are functions built into Windows that can be used to read, write, and update these files, though some argue that they are much slower than using a binary format.

The use of binary format will generally provide more compact files, faster access, and reduce resource requirements. However, unless the file size is extremely large, these are unlikely to be deciding factors in choice of format. It is more likely that software manufacturers choose the binary format to hide the configuration data, and prevent users from fiddling with the settings and breaking the application.

Validating Configuration Files

Preventing application errors, especially where users may be able to edit the configuration data outside the controlled environment (for example, in a text editor instead of from within the application), is extremely important. One way to detect or prevent errors is to validate the configuration data before using it.

Validating files in the INI file format is hard, particularly checking to see if specific values are within a given range or checking that only a specific set of values is present, as there are no proper functions built into Windows to do this. In fact, if the file is not in the correct format (perhaps containing illegal characters or section breaks), the Windows functions that read INI files may not be able to access it at all. And even if they can, the only way you can validate the contents is to read every value you expect to be in there, and check that it meets any conditions you apply for that value. You can't detect if extra entries or sections have been added.

78

Almost the opposite case exists for binary data formats. In general, you have to read all the data and ensure that it fits the pattern required and understood by your application. If it has become corrupted, the individual values may be out of bounds, or the file length may be wrong. The application can check every value, detect errors, and prevent extra values being added to the file.

Plain Text XML Wins

The previous discussions on the two legacy configuration data formats suggest that the ideal file format would have to be:

❑ **Machine-readable**
So that the application can use the data

❑ **Human-readable** (and possibly self-documenting)
So that errors can be detected and repairs made without requiring special tools, even in extreme circumstances where there is no other option, and no suitable backup available

❑ **Structured and extensible**
So that it can be adapted to meet new standards and incorporate new features in the future

❑ **Easy to validate**
So that the configuration file can be validated without the need to always write validation code within the application

XML meets all these requirements. It can be read as a text string and parsed by the application using relatively simple techniques. Alternatively, it can be loaded into an XML parser that is instantiated by the application and accessed using standard XML code techniques. However, XML is also easy for humans to read and understand, especially in the way that it permits values to be nested in a hierarchy that indicates the structuring of the content. Most XML viewers (such as the Internet Explorer) can expand and contract nodes to make it easy to see what the file contains.

XML is also an industry standard that is operating system, application platform, and language agnostic. So there are plenty of specialist and generic tools available for working with it. It also means that the format is extremely unlikely to become isolated or obsolete in the future, as it enjoys such wide support and is proving to be fully capable of accomplishing all the tasks we dream up for it.

Finally, XML provides a huge advantage in that it can be validated in a structured and standard way using **XML Schemas**. Schemas can be used to specify the structure of the file (which elements can appear where, what attributes they can have, how elements can be nested, etc). They can also be used to specify the *values* that can appear for the elements and attributes for example what data type they represent, the maximum and minimum values, individual enumerated values, etc.

*XML documents can also be validated using a **Document Type Definition** (**DTD**). However, these cannot provide anywhere near the same level of detailed control over the format and content, and are generally being superceded by XML Schemas in current and new applications.*

The XML Metabase in IIS

In IIS 6.0, Microsoft has moved to an XML format for the configuration data. The advantages this provides are:

- ❑ The data is in human-readable format; and, if required, can be edited and modified using a simple text editor

- ❑ The data can be validated to ensure that it will not cause runtime errors, and matches the requirements of IIS

- ❑ The configuration data can be easily backed up and restored, and imported and exported

- ❑ The format can be extended in the future, without breaking existing versions

After installation of IIS 6.0, the configuration data resides in two files, they are:

- ❑ `MBSchema.xml`
  This file contains the definition of the configuration file data, as an XML Schema

- ❑ `MetaBase.xml`
  This file contains the configuration data itself

These files are located in the `\Windows\System32\inetsrv\` folder.

> **Note that you must be logged on using an account that has Administrator permissions to be able to view or modify these files, or view them under the context of an account that has Administrator permissions.**

Metabase Backup Files

The installation program also makes a backup copy of the initial configuration in a subfolder of the `inetsrv` folder named `MetaBack`. This consists of two files named `Initial Backup`; the configuration data file having the file extension `MD1` and the schema having the file extension `SC1`.

IIS 6.0 also makes periodical backups of the metabase data and schema in a subfolder of the inetsrv folder named History. These files are named in the following format:

MBSchema_[*majorver*]_[*minorver*].xml and
MetaBase_[*majorver*]_[*minorver*].xml

Where *majorver* is the incremental version number of the metabase and *minorver* is zero. Here is an example:

```
MBSchema_0000000172_0000000000.xml
MetaBase_0000000172_0000000000.xml
```

IIS 6.0 creates a pair of backup files in the History subfolder at regular intervals. Each change to the live configuration files (in the inetsrv folder) causes the current files to be copied to the History folder, using the current version number as shown above, before the live file is replaced by an updated version (which, of course, contains the next version number). Only the last ten schemas and the last ten data files are retained and any previous ones are automatically removed.

The live configuration files are updated in the following scenarios:

❏ Periodically when the configuration has been changed; be it through the **IIS Manager** MMC snap-in, scripts, or other remote administration tools, or programmatic techniques (we'll see these in the next chapter)

❏ When IIS is stopped, if the configuration has been changed since the last time the files were updated

In pre-release versions, IIS also backs up the metabase files when it starts, though this behavior is not documented. In most cases, only the configuration data (and not the schema) will change as you administer IIS. This means that only the live MetaBase.xml file needs to be updated. However, both the MetaBase.xml and MBSchema.xml files are backed up into the History folder each time the configuration changes, irrespective of whether the schema has changed or not.

Documented information suggests that, to reduce the time taken to shut down the service, IIS does not update the configuration files if the configuration of IIS has not been changed since it was started the last time. However, in pre-release versions, the History files are updated every time IIS is restarted, irrespective of whether the configuration has been changed.

We will discuss the administration related tasks in the next chapter using both the IIS Manager and programmatically.

How IIS 6.0 manages the Metabase

The configuration files are XML, but IIS does not handle them simply by using an XML parser to expose the content to its internal routines. There are a couple of reasons for this:

❑ Microsoft wanted existing scripts and applications that manipulate the IIS metabase (for example, administration scripts, applications setup and installation programs, LDAP query applications, etc) to continue to work with IIS 6.0. This means that IIS 6.0 must expose the same programmatic interfaces as IIS 5 for accessing and manipulating the metabase content.

❑ Updating disk-based text files is an error-prone operation; particularly when it may have to survive multiple concurrent updates from administrators using scripts, the IIS Manager, and other utilities, to update the configuration. Instead, the data is best stored and exposed through an in-memory database style structure, as in IIS 5 and earlier.

To achieve these aims, IIS 6.0 uses the process shown in the following diagram to read, store, and manage the metabase data:

Figure1

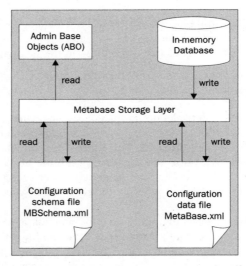

A set of COM objects, called the **Admin Base Objects (ABO)**, is used to manipulate the in-memory database. These objects can be instantiated from within any language or platform that supports COM components, providing a universal way for applications, services, scripts, and other interface systems to manipulate the metabase. Some of these are **Active Directory Services Interface (ADSI)**, **Windows Management Instrumentation (WMI)**, the Internet Information Services snap-in itself, the HTML IIS remote manager web site pages, setup and installation programs, and custom applications that you write or purchase from third-party suppliers.

In the next chapter, we will discuss remote configuration and management of IIS 6.0 through the HTML remote manager web site pages, ADSI, and WMI.

The disk-based XML files that store the configuration data are read and updated through a separate "layer" called the **Metabase Storage Layer**. This is not designed to be accessed programmatically. It simply provides the interface between ABO, the in-memory database, and the disk files.

Metabase Compatibility with IIS 5

By providing the configuration and persistence model that we saw in the earlier schematic, Microsoft has ensured that the new metabase management and storage features in IIS 6.0 are compatible with earlier versions of IIS.

The interfaces to the in-memory database provided by the ABO mean that your existing IIS 5.0 code routines, scripts, and applications would continue to work with IIS 6.0. In effect the new metabase system is abstracted into the Metabase Storage Layer, so externally the system looks identical to IIS 5 and earlier.

The XML Metabase File Format

The XML metabase file is large and quite complex, as it has to contain all the configuration information for IIS. This does, of course, include data for every web site, FTP site, all other services including SMTP service and NNTP. In this section of the chapter we'll look at it in outline to help you understand what it contains, how it is stored, and where to look to find specific items. We don't have room for a full reference to every element in the file, though you can find more information from the IIS Help file in the section Internet Information Services | Server | Administration Guide | IIS Metabase | Metabase Structure or at http://msdn.microsoft.com/library/default.asp?url=/library/en-us/iisref60/htm/mb_aboutmetabase.asp.

We'll start with a look at the overall file structure, followed by some of the more important sections within the file.

The Outline Structure of the File

The MetaBase.xml file contains the root element named <configuration>, within which is a single element named <MBProperty>. Within this element are a series of different types of element, each of which describes a specific property of the current IIS configuration. These properties are referred to as **keys**, and each one is identified by a Location attribute that equates to the LDAP or ADSI schema location path for that key. This is the path used to access the key and change its properties programmatically when using ADSI, WMI, and other tools. The key name (for example IIsComputer) is the name of the ABO class file that you use to manipulate the key values.

The next listing shows the start of the `MetaBase.xml` file, and you can see in the `<IIS_Global>` element the timestamp and change number (the current configuration version number), plus the current number of the history file that this configuration equates to. Other values are included to ensure that the correct version of the `MBSchema.xml` file is used to validate the configuration data in this file:

```
<?xml version="1.0" ?>
  <configuration xmlns="urn:microsoft-catalog:XML_Metabase_V54_0">
    <MBProperty>
      <IIS_Global Location="."
                  BINSchemaTimeStamp="622328805dbdc201"
                  ChangeNumber="1550"
                  HistoryMajorVersionNumber="195"
                  SessionKey="49634b6...63d84"
                  XMLSchemaTimeStamp="0c312b805dbdc201" />

      <IIS_ROOT Location="/"
                AdminACL="49634...7d94" />

      <IIsComputer Location="/LM"
                   EnableEditWhileRunning="0"
                   EnableHistory="1"
                   MaxHistoryFiles="10" />
```

Note that we have formatted all the listing from the MetaBase.xml *file shown in this chapter by adding carriage returns and spaces, to make it easier to see what they contain.*

The listing also shows a couple of the other keys that appear at the start of the file, and define the root properties for the IIS 6.0 service and the computer on which it is running. The hashed versions of the security **Access Control Lists** (ACLs) are included, and basic details about the way IIS should handle metabase file editing, and the history files it creates. You can change the number of history files that are maintained by IIS by editing the value of the `MaxHistoryFiles` attribute here.

The IIS Web (WWW) Service

The IIS 6.0 web service configuration appears as a key named `IIsWebService`. It contains a large number of attributes specifying the values or settings that are global to the web service; and which are inherited by each web site unless they are configured otherwise at site level. The next listing shows a selection of the attributes of the `<IIsWebService>` element with their default values. Most should be immediately apparent from their name:

```
<IIsWebService Location="/LM/W3SVC"
               AllowKeepAlive="TRUE"
               AnonymousUserName="IUSR_SUNDIVE"
               ...
```

```
...
AspSessionTimeout="20"
ConnectionTimeout="120"
ContentIndexed="TRUE"
DefaultDoc=
        "Default.htm,Default.asp,index.htm,Default.aspx"
HttpErrors=
        "400,*,FILE,D:\WINDOWS\help\iisHelp\common\400.htm
        401,1,FILE,D:\WINDOWS\help\iisHelp\common\401-1.htm
        ... etc ... "
LogFileDirectory="D:\WINDOWS\system32\LogFiles"
ScriptMaps=".asa,
        D:\WINDOWS\system32\inetsrv\asp.dll,3,GET,HEAD,POST
    .asax, D:\WINDOWS\..aspnet_isapi.dll,7,GET,HEAD,POST
    ... etc ..."
</IIsWebService>
```

As an example, the attribute named HttpErrors defines the list of error pages, as seen in the Custom Errors page of the Properties dialog for a web site:

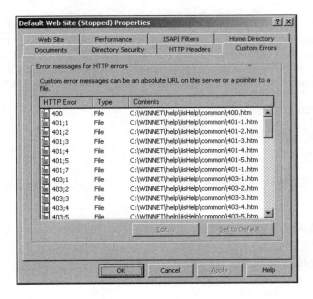

The ScriptMaps attribute shows the script mappings as seen in the Application Configuration dialog of a web site:

85

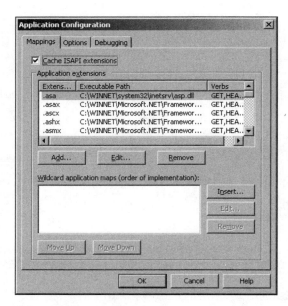

There is a separate key (element) named <IIsWebServer>, which contains details of the settings for the web service itself. For example, it defines the list of default documents that will be sent to the client when they access a directory without specifying a filename, the port that server listens on, and a few other settings:

```
<IIsWebServer Location="/LM/W3SVC/1"
              AppPoolId="DefaultAppPool"
              DefaultDoc
                  ="Default.htm,Default.asp,index.htm,Default.aspx"
              ServerAutoStart="TRUE"
              ServerBindings=":80:"
              ServerComment="Default Web Site"
              ServerSize="1" />
```

Virtual and Web Directories

Within each web site, you can configure one or more virtual directories and virtual applications (application roots). Details of these are stored as a series of <IIsWebVirtualDir> elements. For example, the following section of the MetaBase.xml file shows the configuration for the Default Application that is created for the Default Web Site when you install IIS 6.0:

```
<IIsWebVirtualDir Location="/LM/W3SVC/1/ROOT"
                  AccessFlags="AccessRead | AccessScript"
                  AppFriendlyName="Default Application"
                  AppIsolated="2"
                  AppPoolId="DefaultAppPool"
                  AppRoot="/LM/W3SVC/1/ROOT"
                  Path="C:\Inetpub\wwwroot" />
```

You can see how these settings are reflected in the Properties dialog for the Default Web Site:

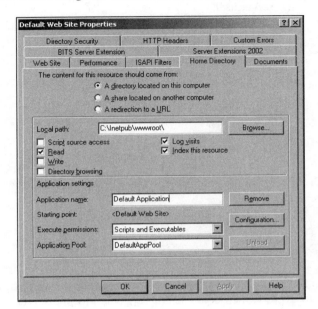

Other, non-application directories are also stored in the configuration file. Remember that you can set the properties of non-application directories, such as specifying the access that the user should have (for example, Read, Write, Directory Browsing):

```
<IIsWebDirectory Location="/LM/W3SVC/1/ROOT/aspnet_client"
                 AccessFlags="AccessRead"
                 DirBrowseFlags="0" />
```

MIME-Type Mappings

The MetaBase.xml file contains a key defining the MIME-type mappings. It specifies the MIME-type that the server should set in the HTTP headers for the response, depending on the file extension of the resource that is requested. A sample of this element is shown next:

```
<IIsMimeMap Location="/LM/MimeMap"
            MimeMap=".asx,video/x-ms-asf
                    .xml,text/xml
                    .tsv,text/tab-separated-values
                    ...
                    .html,text/html
                    .htm,text/html" />
```

This corresponds to the settings in the MIME Types dialog that is accessed from the Properties dialog for the server itself:

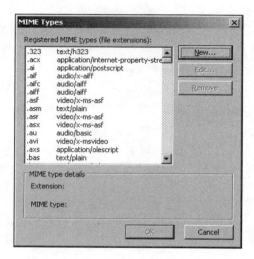

MIME-types can also be specified for each web site, using the MIME Types button in the Properties dialog, to override the default settings specified for the server:

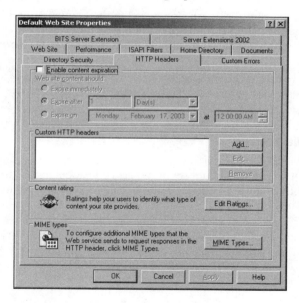

This adds a `MimeMap` attribute to the corresponding `<IIsWebVirtualDir>` element, demonstrating how overrides to the default configuration settings for a specific site or service are stored in the `MetaBase.xml` file:

```
<IIsWebVirtualDir Location="/LM/W3SVC/1/ROOT"
                  AccessFlags="AccessRead | AccessScript"
                  AppFriendlyName="Default Application"
                  AppIsolated="2"
                  AppPoolId="DefaultAppPool"
                  AppRoot="/LM/W3SVC/1/ROOT"
                  MimeMap=".new,New MIME Type Mapping"
                  Path="C:\Inetpub\wwwroot" />
```

The FTP Service

As a second example of the services provided by IIS 6.0, the next listing shows the way that the MetaBase.xml file stores the current configuration of the FTP service. The <IIsFtpService> key contains a series of attributes that hold the values for the various options that are configurable for the FTP service:

```
<IIsFtpService
    Location ="/LM/MSFTPSVC"
    AdminACL="496344...56fc5"
    AllowAnonymous="TRUE"
    AnonymousOnly="FALSE"
    AnonymousUserName="IUSR_TESTWINDOTNET"
    AnonymousUserPass="496344...cfe8488"
    ConnectionTimeout="120"
    DownlevelAdminInstance="1"
    ExitMessage=" "
    LogAnonymous="FALSE"
    LogExtFileFlags="LogExtFileTime | LogExtFileClientIp |
                     LogExtFileMethod | LogExtFileUriStem |
                     LogExtFileHttpStatus |
                     LogExtFileWin32Status"
    LogFileDirectory="C:\WINDOWS\system32\LogFiles"
    LogFilePeriod="1"
    LogFileTruncateSize="20971520"
    LogNonAnonymous="FALSE"
    LogOdbcDataSource="TSLOG"
    LogOdbcPassword="4963446...c00048"
    LogOdbcTableName="FTPLog"
    LogOdbcUserName="InternetAdmin"
    LogPluginClsid="{FF160663-DE82-11CF-BC0A-00AA006111E0}"
    LogType="1"
    MSDOSDirOutput="TRUE"
    MaxClientsMessage=" "
    MaxConnections="100000"
/>
```

You can see that these values reflect the settings in the Properties dialog that opens from the FTP Sites entry in Internet Information Services Manager:

The following dialog box appears on clicking the Properties tab on the previous screen. It displays the path of the log file, which was set by the metabase property LogFileDirectory:

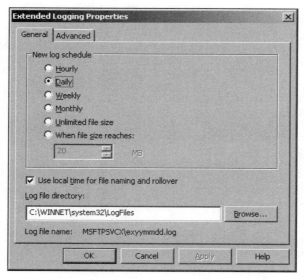

Like the web service, there are keys that define the values for other properties of the service. For example, the <IIsFtpServer> key defines the port number and other details, and the <IIsFtpInfo> key defines the list of logging types available, and the version number of the FTP service:

```
<IIsFtpServer  Location="/LM/MSFTPSVC/1"
               ServerBindings=":21:"
               ServerComment="Default FTP Site"
               ServerSize="1" />

<IIsFtpInfo    Location="/LM/MSFTPSVC/Info"
               LogModuleList="Microsoft IIS Log File Format,W3C
               Extended Log File Format,ODBC Logging"
               MD_SERVER_CAPABILITIES="80831"
               MD_SERVER_PLATFORM="1"
               MajorIIsVersionNumber="6"
               MinorIIsVersionNumber="0" />
```

One or more `<IIsFtpVirtualDir>` keys define the virtual FTP root directories. The next listing shows the default virtual root for the `inetpub\ftproot` folder:

```
<IIsFtpVirtualDir Location="/LM/MSFTPSVC/1/ROOT"
                  AccessFlags="AccessRead"
                  Path="C:\Inetpub\ftproot" />
```

A similar principle is employed for other services installed into IIS 6.0; for example, the **SMTP** and the **NNTP** services. We haven't listed the keys from the `MetaBase.xml` file for these, but you can open this file in Internet Explorer and view the contents.

Access Logging Configuration

Other keys in the `MetaBase.xml` file define further details of how IIS is configured, demonstrating just how flexible and extensible it actually is. For example, all the details of the custom logging formats available for the various services are stored as a series of `<IIsCustomLogModule>` elements. The following one shows the key that defines the `Bytes Received` column in custom logging mode:

```
<IIsCustomLogModule
    LogCustomPropertyNodeID="17"
    Location="/LM/Logging/Custom Logging/Extended Properties/Bytes
            Received"
    LogCustomPropertyDataType="3"
    LogCustomPropertyHeader="cs-bytes"
    LogCustomPropertyMask="8192"
    LogCustomPropertyName="Bytes Received" />
```

General Configuration Objects

The XML Schema for the `MetaBase.xml` file allows this file to contain multiple `<IIsConfigObject>` elements. Unlike all the other elements in the file, these special keys are not uniquely identified by the element name. Instead, the value of the `Location` attribute must be unique for each one. These elements can be used to define custom properties, which are not tied to any specific section or service within IIS 6.0:

```
<IIsConfigObject Location="..." />
<IIsConfigObject Location="/LM/EventManager/SourceTypes" />
```

Secure Encrypted Properties

The XML Schema file (MBSchema.xml) defines all of the property types that are used in the keys in the MetaBase.xml configuration data file. Each of the property definitions has an Attributes attribute that specifies how the property value (which is held in an attribute of the key element in MetaBase.xml) should behave. Amongst the values for this definition is SECURE, which instructs IIS to encrypt the value of the property when it persists it to disk in the MetaBase.xml file.

By default, the encryption takes place with a blank password, allowing any members of the Administrators group to restore the configuration from these files. However, this still prevents users, who might browse the file, from viewing the content of these secure properties. It is also possible to encrypt the secure property values when backing up the configuration, using a password that you specify, as we'll see in the sections on backing up and restoring the configuration later in this chapter.

Schema Extensibility

As we've seen, the data required to set up the configuration of IIS 6.0 is persisted to disk in the file named MetaBase.xml. The content of this file changes as the configuration of IIS 6.0 changes. However, even though it is backed up along with MetaBase.xml, the content of the "other" configuration file (MBSchema.xml) changes very rarely.

MBSchema.xml holds the schema that defines the structure and permissible content for the MetaBase.xml file. Therefore, the only time that the MBSchema.xml file will change is when the actual setup of the IIS 6.0 service (rather than the configuration of existing services) is changed, for example when a new service is installed.

The advantage is that this allows the configuration schema to adapt as required, and be extended to include other configuration settings that are necessary. As IIS 6.0 is upgraded, patched or extended in the future (perhaps through service packs, O/S upgrades, etc), the schema can change to match the requirements of IIS 6.0.

Corrupted Metabase Files

IIS 6.0 reads the MetaBase.xml configuration file when it first starts up, and also after a restart. It validates the content of this file against the current XML Schema defined in the matching file MBSchema.xml. Providing that the MetaBase.xml file content is well-formed (in other words, it is correctly formed and delimited in line with the W3C "rules" for XML) and is valid, when compared with the schema definition, the data is read into the in-memory database and used to set up IIS 6.0.

However, if the file is not well formed, or contains invalid elements or data, IIS will not be able to use it. In this case, an event is written to the System Event Log indicating the problem:

When an invalid metabase XML file is encountered, IIS will attempt to recover automatically by reverting to a previous version of the configuration using the history files. If this occurs, you can recover by restoring the "last known good" metabase from the history file of your choice (in the `History` subfolder); or in the worst case scenario, from the `Initial Backup` files containing the configuration of the metabase when IIS was installed. These are in the `MetaBack` sub-folder. We will look at the process of restoring a previous backup of the metabase later in this chapter.

If the metabase file is not well formed, IIS may fail to start altogether, and IIS Manager will not be able to connect to the server. The System event log will show the error details, and you can recover the previous configuration by copying the most recent configuration files from the `History` or `MetaBack` folder and renaming them to `MetaBase.xml` and `MBSchema.xml`.

Editing the Configuration Data

As far as configuring IIS 6.0 is concerned, little has changed over IIS 5. There are, of course, new features in IIS 6.0 (for example, application pools), but in general the whole thing will be familiar to users of IIS 5. Moreover, as the configuration persistence model is abstracted from the IIS Manager MMC console, you don't need to be aware of how the metabase data is stored.

However, Microsoft has provided the facility to directly edit the configuration files, if this is required. There is an option to allow them to be edited even while IIS is running. In the Properties dialog for the computer (here named DOTNETSERVER), set the Enable Direct Metabase Edit option:

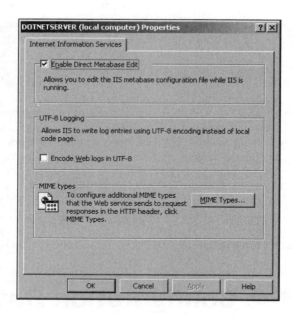

While it is possible to manually edit the MetaBase.xml file, not setting this option can result in loss of data. You should always set this option before editing the MetaBase.xml file; otherwise, the changes made to the configuration while IIS is running may be lost when restarting.

Microsoft suggests that the option for manual editing of the MetaBase.xml file is only intended for administrators, who do not want to use the ABO or other programmatic techniques to update the configuration of IIS. It is also faster than programmatic editing, and may be a useful option for administering IIS over a slow network connection. The MetaBase.xml file could also be updated using FTP. However, this requires the FTP user account to have administrative rights, and access to the inetsrv folder on the server, both of which could expose a security risk.

Microsoft strongly advises against editing the XML Schema file MBSchema.xml at any time, whether IIS is running or not.

How the Direct Edit Feature works

When you enable direct editing of the MetaBase.xml file, IIS uses the file change notification feature built into Windows to detect any changes to the file. It then performs a series of checks to see if the current configuration version in the in-memory database matches the version number in the updated configuration file. If they match, and there are no errors detected in the MetaBase.xml file, it instructs the ABOs to update the in-memory database with the changed values in the MetaBase.xml file.

At the same time, IIS saves the previous configuration to the `History` sub-folder, to allow rollback to the previous settings, in the case of an error. The combined process ensures that the changes made to the `MetaBase.xml` file are persisted when the in-memory configuration data is saved to disk next time.

Points to Note

There are a few things to be aware of with the new system of configuration persistence, some of which are just a matter of general "good practice":

Use runas to Gain Administrative Privileges

Rather than logging onto the server with an account that has administrative permissions, it is safer to log on with your usual "user-level" account and then use the `runas` command to gain administrative privileges only when you require them. For example, when you want to edit the `MetaBase.xml` file directly.

In the Start menu, right-click on the program you want to run (for example, IIS Manager) and select Run As. In the Run As dialog, specify an account with administrative permission that you want to use:

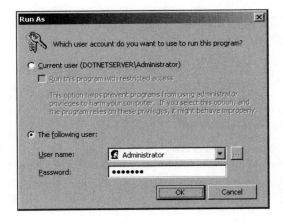

Alternatively, you can run programs from the Command Prompt. You will be prompted for the password for the account you specify.

Disabling History File Creation

It's possible to change the way that IIS maintains the history files in the `History` sub-folder. You can control the number of files that are kept in this by changing the value of the `MaxHistoryFiles` attribute in the `IIsComputer` element from its default value of `10`:

```
<IIsComputer Location="/LM"
             EnableEditWhileRunning="0"
             EnableHistory="1"
             MaxHistoryFiles="25" />
```

You can also turn off the "history feature" altogether, by changing the value of the `EnableHistory` attribute to zero:

```
<IIsComputer Location="/LM"
             EnableEditWhileRunning="0"
             EnableHistory="0"
             MaxHistoryFiles="25" />
```

However, this should be avoided unless you have sufficient back-up copies of the configuration files, or you maintain some custom centralized system for backing up the configuration files. If the main `MetaBase.xml` configuration file should become corrupted or lost, IIS will need to be completely reconfigured from an "empty" state.

History File Security

All the copies of `MetaBase.xml` and `MBSchema.xml` files in the `History` and `MetaBack` sub-folders have ACLs set up to only allow them to be read and updated by accounts that are members of the Administrators group, or the SYSTEM account under which IIS 6.0 runs. While you can change these permissions, it is not recommended, as they contain sensitive information about the configuration of your server, including the ACLs that are specified for user access to the services. If you copy the history files to another location, or back them up onto tape or other backup media, make sure that the ACLs are preserved to protect the files from "general" unsecured access.

Some values in the MetaBase.xml file are stored in encrypted form, and these cannot be edited directly. Only ADSI, WMI, or the ABOs can be used to update encrypted property values.

To monitor direct physical edits and other changes to the MetaBase.xml file, you can use Windows built-in auditing feature. Right-click on the file, select Properties, and click the Advanced button in the Security page. In the dialog that appears, you can add auditing entries for the file to monitor specific users, or better still, whole account groups:

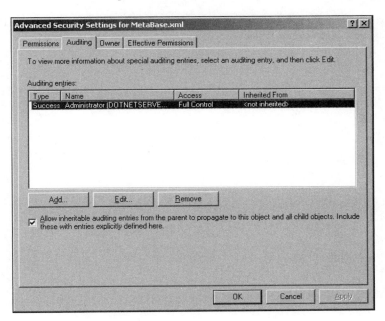

Summary

In this chapter, we've looked at the way that IIS 6.0 provides a completely new and more robust method for persisting the configuration of the server. Rather than using a proprietary format, the metabase details are stored in XML format in two disk files. One contains an XML Schema that defines the configuration data format (MBSchema.xml) and the other contains the data itself (MetaBase.xml).

To provide better recoverability from errors, as well as a "history" log, IIS keeps the last ten versions of these two files in a separate History folder, and you can restore the configuration of IIS from any of these. The history files are saved at intervals when IIS is running and when the configuration is changed (using IIS Manager, the HTML remote management pages, or any other programmatic methods). It is also saved when IIS starts successfully, and when it is closed down or restarted.

The configuration data file can be edited manually, or the configuration of IIS can be managed by any of the existing techniques used with earlier versions of IIS. A set of **Admin Base Objects** (ABO) that is compatible with the earlier versions of IIS can be used to read and edit the in-memory database that implements the metabase at runtime.

There are tools and scripts provided that you can use to backup and restore the metabase on demand, or import and export specific subsets of the configuration data (for example, a specific web site or web application).

In the next chapter, we move on to look at administering IIS 6.0 by using the IIS Manager as well as programmatically.

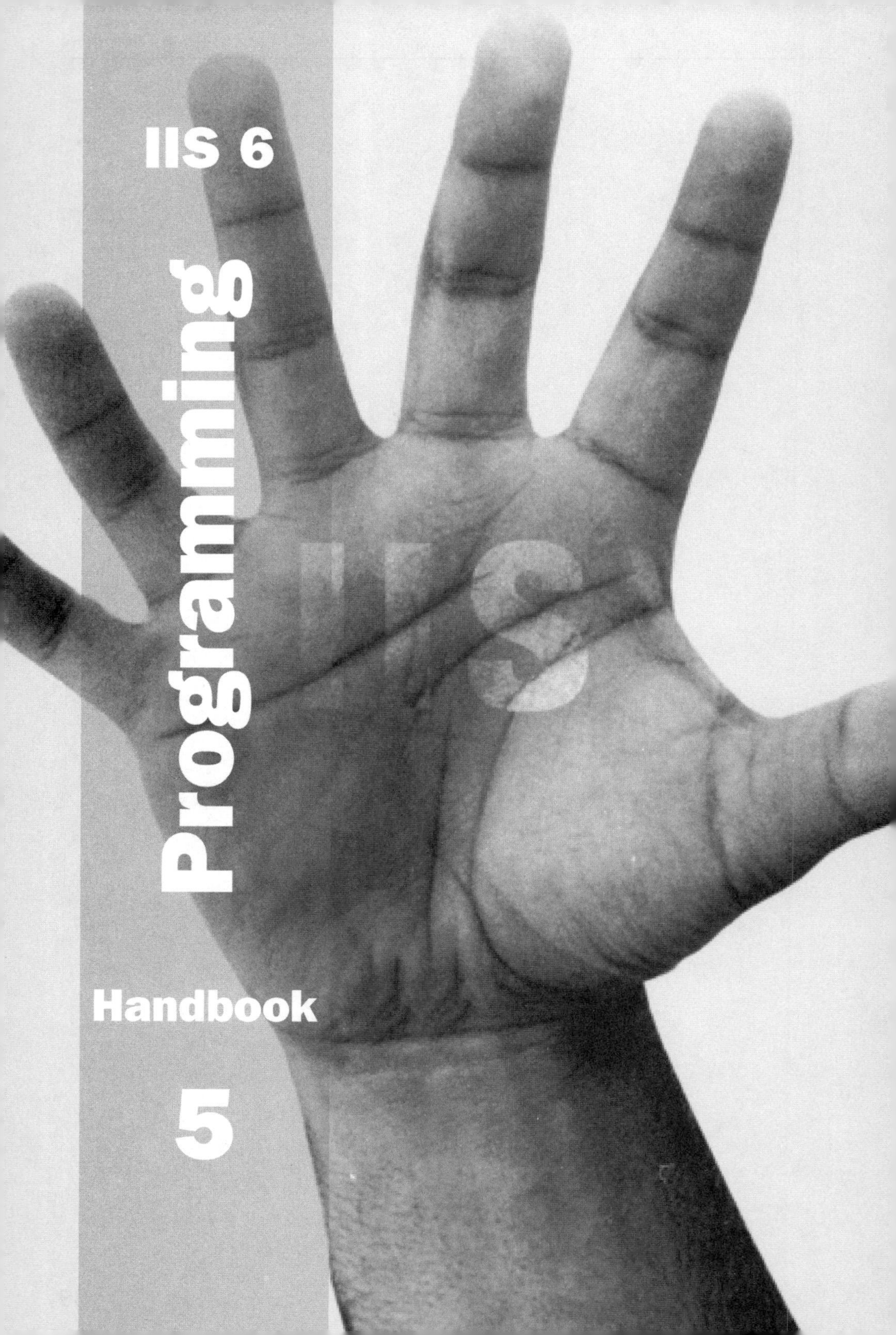
IIS 6
Programming
Handbook
5

5

Administering IIS 6.0

Let's face it. Administration is not an easy task. Any server platform that you choose needs lot of attention and manual administration work. There is no magic about it. When you are hosting busy web sites, FTP sites, or news sites, you have to go a long way to make sure they are running smoothly without any trouble. It is very difficult to possibly predict and prevent all the breakdowns or potential issues that can happen on the server side. However, we can take a few administrative steps that can ensure that the server runs as smoothly as expected. The basic concept behind the administration is that, when you manage the IIS services using code, scripts, or MMC, it also changes the underlying metabase. In this chapter we'll learn all about IIS 6.0 server administration. In particular, we'll discuss the following:

❑   Command line administration

❑   Programmatic administration

❑   Remote administration

❑   Configuring Quality of Service

We can administer IIS using a number of tools and the options have been growing from one IIS version to another. In the initial versions of IIS, we had MMC. However, the later version has evolved a lot and given us more options, including the use of scripts. In this section, we'll see the IIS administration options.

MMC

MMC (or **Microsoft Management Console**) is the most famous way to administrate. MMC hasn't changed a lot in IIS 6.0 when compared to version 5 other than a few new options. The biggest change is the XML-based metabase (as discussed in the previous chapter). In this chapter we'll cover the newer features of IIS. We'll discuss IIS 6.0 MMC wherever necessary.

Command Line Administration

Command line administration is very popular among administrators. It makes administration easy, more productive, and allows administrators to do the tasks with a simple command rather than clicking on a couple of menus and user interface elements to achieve the same. The other advantage of using the command line is that they can be a part of a script that can be used to automate tasks or even remote administration. This is true with any server software including IIS.

Unlike previous versions of IIS, IIS 6.0 includes good support for command line administration.

What can we do with the command line?

IIS 6.0 includes a few command line scripts that can be used to administer IIS 6.0 and previous versions of IIS servers, including administration of all the IIS services such as HTTP, FTP, NNTP, and SMTP. We'll learn about these options in this session.

All the IIS command line scripts are written in VBScript and they can only be executed with administrator privilege. All the command line scripts are stored under the Windows/System32 folder. The VBScript utilities are written using the **Windows Management Instrumentation** (**WMI**) provider. We'll learn about WMI in the *WMI* section.

> *The VBScript command line utility can run using the CScript.exe file. The CScript.exe is the command line version of the **Windows Scripting Host**.*

The command line utilities allow you to list, add, modify, delete, start, stop, and pause IIS services such as web sites, virtual directories, FTP service, etc.

To keep the risk minimal, it is strongly recommended that you always log on to the Windows Servers using a normal un-prevailed account. When you need to run an application or a utility with admin privileges then use the Run as option in the menu:

Or the RunAs command-line utility:

```
C:>RunAs /user:AdminAccount "Command".
```

> **Since we're dealing with IIS 6.0 here, it is also highly recommended that you store all the Admin scripts in a place where it is unreachable from the Internet (that is, to store them away from the WWW folders and IIS virtual folder). Assign tight ACL's on those files so that only Administrators can access those scripts.**

Even though the documentation suggests we use the RunAs command, it is not available for non-executable files such as the Admin VBScript functions. The best way to address this problem is to use the RunAs command to open a new command shell with admin privileges. Here is an example:

```
C:>RunAs /User:Administrator "Cmd /k"
```

When we include the /k command line argument, a new command shell will be opened. This shell will not close until the user closes it explicitly.

```
C:\WINDOWS\system32\cmd.exe                                           _□×

C:\Documents and Settings\nileshp>runas /user:administrator "cmd /k"
Enter the password for administrator:
Attempting to start cmd /k as user "DOTNETSERVER\administrator" ...

C:\Documents and Settings\nileshp>
```

```
cmd /k (running as DOTNETSERVER\administrator)                        _□×

C:\WINDOWS\system32>iisweb /Query
Connecting to server ...Done.
Site Name (Metabase Path)              Status   IP          Port  Host
===================================================================
Default Web Site (W3SVC/1)             STARTED ALL          80    N/A
Default Web Site (W3SVC/5)             STOPPED ALL          80    N/A

C:\WINDOWS\system32>
```

The Net Command

The Net command comes to Windows OS from the **Microsoft LAN Manager** days. The Windows Servers provide an extended set of commands that can be effectively used in batch files to automate network-related tasks. One such command is the Net command. The Net command was basically a single command that could be used to accomplish a wide variety of network-related tasks, such as logging in or mapping a network drive. The Net command is always a two-part command. The first part comprises of the command itself, and then the parameters follow. For example, the Net computer command allows you to add a computer account to or remove a computer account from a domain. The best thing about this command is that if you have a list of computer account names you can write a simple batch file to add or remove those account names.

We can also use the Net command to manage any Windows service including starting, stopping, and pausing IIS services such as World Wide Web Publishing Service, FTP Publishing Service, SMTP, and NNTP.

For example, we can start, stop, and pause the World Wide Web Publishing Service using the following Net command by passing either the service's executable filename or service's display name:

```
C:>Net Start W3svc
```

or

```
C:>Net Start "World Wide Web Publishing Service"
```

Although the Net command allows us to manage the IIS services, it doesn't provide the granular control over how to manage individual IIS elements. For example, let's say we have four web sites running inside IIS 6.0 and we just want to stop one single web site. With the Net command, we can't stop the single web site; instead it will stop the whole IIS web publishing service, as a result stopping all the IIS web sites.

Managing Web Applications

One of the main tasks of the administrator is to monitor the health of the web applications. We can do this by using the IISApp script. This script shows all the running web applications (currently running worker process that is W3wp.exe) with the Process ID (PID) and application pool ID (AppPoolID):

```
C:>IISApp
W3WP.exe  PID: 2040  AppPoolId: DefaultAppPool
```

> *You can also see specific application information either using the process ID (/P) or application pool ID (/A).*

Managing web sites includes tasks such as creating, removing, starting, stopping, pausing and of course querying. All these tasks can be done from the command prompt using the IISWeb.vbs file.

Querying Web Sites

Being an administrator or web developer, you may need to query information about the IIS 6.0 server or health of the web sites running inside the IIS 6.0 server. The /Query command line switch just does that for you. For example, to list all the web sites running on the server, we issue the following command:

The above listing shows information regarding the web site name with the metabase path, status of the web site, the IP address which the web site is hosted on, the port the web site is listening to, and the host header.

> *If you want to get help information about how to use the /Query command line switch you can type "IISWeb /Query /Help".*

Let's say your web server is hosting a number of web sites and you just want to query information of a particular web site, then you can give the web site name as the parameter.

You can also pass the metabase path instead of using the web site's full name.

If you want to query a remote server, then you can use the command line switches as shown below:

❑   /s for the server

❑   /u for the user

❑   /p for the password

If you are not comfortable in typing the password with the /p command line switch then, you can ignore this switch and when the script is executed it'll prompt you for the password.

Starting, Stopping, and Pausing Web Sites

Perhaps the most common tasks of administrators (or developers who are a part of a development team) is having to stop and start a web site due to problems such as a slow or unresponsive site or to maintenance the site. If you do not want to stop the site, which may cause problems with running an existing process, then you can pause it, which will allow the existing processes to run smoothly to its end. Whatever your strategy is, the /Start, /Stop, /Pause command line switches help you achieve this task. To start, stop, or pause a web site, you can simply call the IISWeb script with the web site name:

To stop, start, or pause multiple sites, we need to pass the entire site name or the metabase path as command line arguments. In the same way you can stop, start, or pause web sites running on different server then you can point to the server using /s for server, /u for username and /p for password.

Creating Web Sites

Creating web sites from the command line can be done using the /Create command line switch:

```
C:>IISWeb /Create C:\Inetpub\wwwroot\MyIIS 6.0Site MyIIS 6.0Site
Connecting to server ...Done.
Server        = DOTNETSERVER
Site Name     = MyIIS 6.0Site
Metabase Path = W3SVC/14453
IP            = ALL UNASSIGNED
Host          = NOT SPECIFIED
Port          = 80
Root          = C:\Inetpub\wwwroot\MyIIS 6.0Site
Status        = STARTED
```

We can also use the following switches with the /Create command line switch.

Switch	Description
/b	This switch is uses to assign a port number to the newly created web site.
/i	This switch is used to assign an IP address to the newly created web site.
/d	This switch is used to assign a host header string to the newly created web site.
/dontstart	This indicates that the web site shouldn't start immediately after it is created. For example, while launching a new site, the DNS propagation may take a few days, and during this time you may not want to start the web site. In this kind of scenario the /dontstart is very useful.

Apart from these we can also use the usual command line switches to specify the username (/u), password (/p) and computer (/s). In fact all the admin scripts accept these command line switches.

Even though the /Create switch does a very nice job, it can't do lot of other things that can be done via the IIS MMC. For example, when we create a web site, we can choose what kind of authentication or logging that we want to do. This can be done using the MMC but can't be done with the command line script.

Removing Web Sites

Removing an existing web site from the command line can be done using the /Delete command line switch. The /Delete command line switch only takes one parameter which is the web site name or the metabase path:

```
C:>IISWeb /Delete MyIIS6.0Site
Connecting to server ...Done.
Server W3SVC/14453 has been deleted
```

> When you use the IISWeb script with /Create switch, if the folder doesn't exist then it will be created. However, when you use the /Delete switch to remove the web site the web site mapping from IIS 6 is removed but the physical folder is not removed from the file system.

Managing Virtual Directories

We can also manage the IIS virtual directories as we do the web sites. All the virtual directories can be managed using the IISvDir script. The IISvDir script supports three switches that are /Query, /Create, and /Delete.

For example if you want to query all the virtual directories inside a web site you can do that by passing the site name to the script.

```
C:>IISvDir /Query WroxIIS6.0BookSite
Connecting to server ...Done.

Alias                      Physical Root
===========================================================
/Chapter4                  C:\My Stuff\My Books\Wrox\8392\CH04
/Chapter5                  C:\My Stuff\My Books\Wrox\8392\CH05
```

In the same way, you can create a virtual directory using /Create switch. The following example creates a virtual directory called MyTest in the WroxIIS 6.0BookSite using the /Create switch.

```
C:>IISvDir /Create WroxIIS6.0BookSite MyTest C:\My Stuff\My
Books\Wrox\8392\MyTest
Connecting to server ...Done.
Virtual Path  = WroxIIS6.0BookSite/ROOT/MyTest
ROOT          = C:\My Stuff\My Books\Wrox\8392\MyTest
Metabase Path = W3SVC/1333745956/ROOT/MyTest
```

We can also remove a virtual directory by specifying the path.

```
C:>IISvDir /Delete WroxIIS 6.0BookSite/MyTest
Connecting to server ...Done.
Web directory WroxIIS 6.0BookSite/ROOT/MyTest has been DELETED.
```

Managing FTP Sites

Managing FTP sites from the command line can be done using the `IISFtp.vbs` script file. The `IISFTP` script allows you to query, create, delete, start, stop, and pause the FTP sites. Also, you can configure the "FTP Isolation Level Mode" for the FTP site.

> *The FTP Isolation Level is useful, when the IIS 6.0 server is hosted in a (Internet Service Provider) ISP or ASP (Application Service Provider) scenario, and you want to offer individual directories for FTP or Web upload for each user. The FTP Isolation level can be set for individual FTP sites. The allowed settings are "Do not isolate users", "Isolate users" and "Isolate users using Active Directory".*

As we did with the web sites, we can use the same switches with the `IISFtp.vbs` script file. For example, we can list all the available FTP sites using the `/Query` switch:

```
C:>IISFtp /Query
Connecting to server ...Done.

Site Name (Metabase Path)      Status   IP  Port
=======================================================================
Default FTP Site (MSFTPSVC/1)  STARTED ALL   21
```

We can also start, stop, or pause the FTP sites using the `/Start`, `/Stop` and `/Pause` switches:

We can also create a new FTP site using the `/Create` switch and pass the physical path of the FTP site and the name of the FTP site:

```
C:>IISFtp /Create C:\Inetpub\FTPRoot\WroxBookSite WroxBookSite
Connecting to server ...Done.
Server       = DOTNETSERVER
Site Name    = WroxBookSite
Metabase Path = MSFTPSVC/755766228
IP           = ALL UNASSIGNED
Port         = 21
Root         = C:\Inetpub\FTPRoot\WroxBookSite
Status       = STARTED
```

In the same way, we can delete a FTP site by using the /Delete switch:

```
C:>IISFtp /Delete WroxBookSite
Connecting to server ...Done.
Server MSFTPSVC/755766228 has been DELETED
```

The FTP isolation level always works for user accounts and FTP sites. The isolation level stores and authenticates the user information from the Active Directory. So this is a very minimum requirement to use this feature. To set the user isolation level we have to use the /SetAdProp switch and to retrieve information we use the /GetAdProp switch. Here is an example of how to use the /GetAdProp switch:

```
C:>IISFtp /GetAdProp WROXACCOUNT
Connecting to server ...Done.
Server       = DOTNETSERVER
Site Name    = WroxBookSite
Metabase Path = MSFTPSVC/755766228
IP           = ALL UNASSIGNED
Port         = 21
Root         = C:\Inetpub\FTPRoot\WroxBookSite
IsoMode      = FTPRoot
Status       = STARTED
```

The above example shows how to query the isolation mode for the user account DOTNETSERVER and it provides all the basic server information and the mode of access. The two modes allowed are FTPRoot (the FTP Root folder) and FTPDir (the FTP Virtual Directory).

If we want to set the isolation level for a user we can use the /SetAdProp switch and assign isolation mode FTPRoot or FTPDir. For example, the following command assigns FTPDir mode to the WroxUser.

```
C:>IISFtp /SetAdProp WroxUser FTPDir WroxBookSite
Connecting to server ...Done.
Server       = DOTNETSERVER
Site Name    = WroxBookSite
Metabase Path = MSFTPSVC/755766228
```

```
IP          = ALL UNASSIGNED
Port        = 21
Root        = C:\Inetpub\FTPRoot\WroxBookSite
IsoMode     = FTPRoot
Status      = STARTED
```

Managing FTP Virtual Directories

Like the web virtual directories, the FTP Virtual directories can be managed using the
IISFtpDr.vbs script and it supports querying, creating, removing, and setting up
isolation level. Let's see a few quick samples.

To create a new FTP virtual directory:

```
C:>IISFtpDr /Create WroxBookSite Code
C:\Inetpub\FTPRoot\WroxBookSite\Code
Connecting to server ...Done.
Virtual Path  = WroxBookSite/ROOT/Code
Root          = C:\Inetpub\FTPRoot\WroxBookSite\Code
Metabase Path = MSFTPSVC/755766228/ROOT/Code
```

To query all the virtual directories inside a FTP site, we use the following command:

```
C:>IISFtpDr /Query WroxBookSite
Connecting to server ...Done.
Alias         Physical Root
==========================
/Code         C:\Inetpub\FTPRoot\WroxBookSite\Code
```

To remove a FTP virtual directory:

```
C:>IISFtp /Delete WroxBookSite/Code
Connecting to server ...Done.
FTP directory WroxBookSite/ROOT/Code has been DELETED
```

> *The isolation level can be set using the* IISFTP *script with the*
> FTPDir *parameter.*

Managing IIS Configuration

As we all know, IIS 6.0 stores all the configuration information in XML files. We also
know how important it is to take a backup of the configuration information in timely
fashion to avoid any unexpected failures. Moreover, it is always recommended that we
take a backup of the current configuration information before changing configuration
of the server.

All IIS configuration can be done using the `IISBack.vbs` and `IISCnfg.vbs` script files. In this section we'll learn how to manage the IIS 6.0 configuration information from the command line.

We have seen how the new configuration persistence features of IIS 6.0 work, what they do, and how you can edit the disk files manually. Now, we'll look at the way you can backup and restore configuration data. Later, we'll also see how we can export and import subsets of the server configuration as well. There are two approaches to backing up or exporting the configuration of IIS:

❑ Using the menu commands and options in IIS Manager

❑ Using the scripts supplied with IIS 6.0 to back up, restore, export, and import the metabase

We'll look at both approaches, starting with backing up and restoring the configuration using the IIS snap-in to the MMC.

Configuration Backup with IIS Manager

The simplest :way to back up IIS 6.0 is through the IIS Manager. Right-click on the entry for the computer, and select All Tasks:

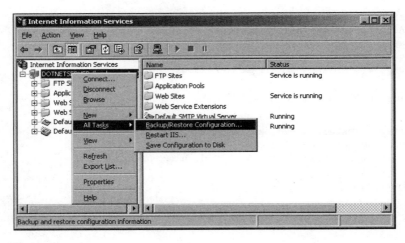

The submenu that appears offers three options:

❑ **Backup/Restore Configuration**
This option can be used to create a pair of files (the metabase schema and the metabase data file) in the `MetaBack` subfolder, or restore the configuration of IIS from an existing pair of such files (either from the `MetaBack` folder, or the automatically generated backups in the `History` subfolder).

112

❏ **Restart IIS**

This provides a series of options for starting, stopping, and restarting IIS or the computer itself.

❏ **Save Configuration to Disk**

This allows you to export the complete configuration of IIS, including details of all installed services, to a file. This option is also available at the FTP Sites, Application Pools, and Web Sites levels in the left hand services tree, and for individual sites or application pools.

Let us discuss each of these in more detail.

Backing Up the Complete Server Configuration

Selecting the Backup/Restore Configuration option shown earlier, brings up a dialog where you can view the existing configuration: backups. This includes the Initial Backup that was created when IIS was installed (in the `MetaBack` subfolder), and the Automatic Backup entries for each of the pairs of files in the `History` subfolder:

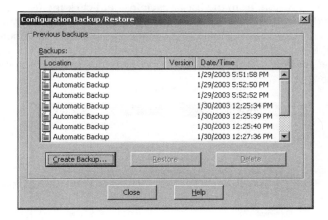

To create a backup, click the Create Backup button in the previous screen to open another dialog where you specify details of the backup:

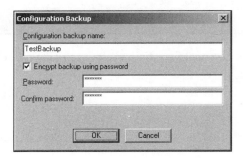

113

This operation creates two files, with the name you specify, in the `MetaBack` subfolder. The schema is saved with the file extension `SC0` and the configuration data with the file extension `MD0`. If you specify a name for the backup that already exists, the files are created with the same name, but the file extensions are incremented, so that the next backup will use `SC1` and `MD1`, and so on.

Encrypting the Backup File

You can encrypt the: backup file by setting the checkbox in the dialog (on the right in the earlier screenshot), and specifying the password to use. This does not encrypt the whole file; it simply encrypts the session keys and "secure" property values within the file using this password. When restoring from this backup, the password must be provided to decrypt these property values.

Restoring the Complete Server Configuration

The Backup/Restore Configuration dialog can also be used to restore an existing backup or history file, should the :current configuration be lost or corrupted. Simply select the backup you want to restore from the list of backups, and click the Restore button. Notice how the dialog shows the "version" of the backups you create yourself (as demonstrated in the previous section). This version number is the number in the file extension (`MD0`, `MD1`, and so on), and allows you to differentiate backups that have the same name. The automatic backups in the `History` folder are shown with the name Automatic Backup:

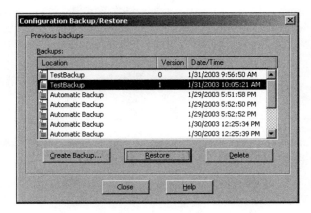

If the backup is encrypted, you'll be prompted for the password to decrypt it before it is restored.

Deleting Backup Files

You can use the Delete button in the Backup/Restore Configuration dialog to remove backups that you have created yourself. However, you cannot delete the history files (named Automatic Backup) this way because IIS manages them itself, as we saw earlier in this chapter.

Programmatic Configuration Backups

IIS 6.0 provides a range of scripts that you can use to:

❑ Back up configurations

❑ Restore configurations

❑ Export configurations

❑ Import configurations

❑ List backup files programmatically

These scripts are located in the Windows\System32 folder, and can be executed within a Command Prompt window or by using the Run command on the Start menu. To backup and restore the configuration of IIS, we use the iisback.vbs script.

Backing up the Complete Server Configuration

The general syntax for the iisback.vbs script when backing up a server is:

```
iisback /backup [/s computer] [/b backup-name] [/v {integer |
HIGHEST_VERSION | NEXT_VERSION}] [/overwrite] [/e encrypt-password]
[/u [domain\]user-name /p password]
```

The parameters for the iisback.vbs script when used for creating a backup are shown in the following table:

Parameter	Example	Description
/s computer	/s dotnetserver	The name or the IP address of the computer to back up. If omitted, the default is the local computer.
/b backup-name	/b dotnerserver	The name of the back up file. If omitted, the name SampleBackup is used.

Table continued on following page

Parameter	Example	Description
/v *version*	/v 15	Either the version number to use for the backup files (the value for the ChangeNumber attribute), the value NEXT_VERSION to use the next version number, or the value HIGHEST_VERSION to replace the most recent backup files. If omitted, the value NEXT_VERSION is assumed.
/overwrite		Instructs IIS to replace any existing backup files with the same version number. Must be used when the /v parameter is HIGHEST_VERSION.
/e *encrypt-password*	/e secret	The password to be used to encrypt the session keys and "secure" values in the backup file.
/u *domain\user*	/u mydomain\admin	The user name to run the script under. Can include the domain if required. The account specified must have administrative privileges on the machine.
/p *password*	/p letmein	The password for the account used to run the script. If omitted, the script prompts for the password when it runs.

As an example, the following screenshot shows the result of executing the iisback command:

You can see the Connecting to server message, and the confirmation that the process was completed successfully. The section below this is the output from a listing of the backup files on the machine, and you can see the new backup file names TestBackup in the list.

To list the backup files on a machine, we use the iisback utility again, but this time with the /list parameter.

As well as specifying the machine name (which can be omitted to list the backups on the local machine), we can specify the user name and password of an account under which the script will run. This uses the same parameters as the /backup option shown earlier.

Restoring the Complete Server Configuration

The general syntax for the iisback.vbs script when restoring a server from backup files is:

```
iisback /restore [/s computer] /b backup-name [/v {integer |
HIGHEST_VERSION}] [/e encrypt-password] [/u [domain\]user-name
/p password]
```

The parameters for the iisback.vbs script when used for restoring the configuration are shown in the following table:

Parameter	Example	Description
/s computer	/s dotnetserver	The name or the IP address of the computer to restore to. If omitted, the default is the local computer.
/b backup-name	/b dotnetserver	The name of the back up file to restore. Required parameter.
/v version	/v 15	Either the version number of the backup files to use (the value for the ChangeNumber or HistoryMajorVersionNumber attribute), or the value HIGHEST_VERSION to use the most recent backup files. If omitted, the value HIGHEST_VERSION is assumed.
/e encrypt-password	/e secret	The password to be used to decrypt the session keys and "secure" values in the backup file.
/u domain\user	/u mydomain\admin	The user name to run the script under. Can include the domain if required. The account specified must have administrative privileges on the machine.
/p password	/p letmein	The password for the account used to run the script. If omitted, the script prompts for the password when it runs.

As an example, the following screenshot shows the result of executing the command:

Again, you can see the Connecting to server message, and the confirmation that the process was completed successfully.

Restarting IIS with IIS Manager

After you perform a restore of the configuration, IIS is restarted automatically. However, you can start, stop, and restart IIS using the menu commands in IIS Manager, and even reboot the server if required. The Restart IIS command (in the same submenu as the Backup/Restore Configuration command) opens a dialog where you specify the action you want to take:

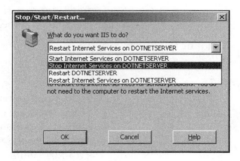

Restarting IIS Programmatically

Alternatively, you can restart IIS using the iisreset.exe utility. In a command window or in the Run dialog type the command, iisreset. This stops and restarts all the IIS services on the local machine. To restart IIS on another networked machine, to which you have Administrator level access, append the name of the machine to the command as shown below:

```
C:> iisreset machine-name
```

The iisreset command can also be used to stop and start all the services, individual services, or reboot the computer. For a list of the options and command line parameters for the iisreset.exe utility and enter:

```
C:> iisreset /?
```

Importing and Exporting Application Data

As well as backing up and restoring the complete configuration of IIS, you can back up and restore subsets of the configuration as a file. This is akin to exporting and importing configuration data, and it provides a way to move or copy configuration details between servers. It can be accomplished by:

❑   Using the menu commands and options in IIS Manager

❑   Using the scripts supplied with IIS 6.0 to export or import configuration subsets programmatically

We'll start by looking at the menu commands in IIS Manager.

Configuration Export and Import with IIS Manager

You can save the configuration of the complete server including all **FTP Sites**, **application pools**, and **web sites**, or an individual FTP site, application pool or web site. Notice that you cannot export the configuration of the SMTP server or the NNTP server separately; this can only be done as part of the complete machine configuration.

Saving the Configuration as a file

To save all or a subset of the IIS configuration to a file, open the IIS Manager and right-click on the entry that corresponds to the section you want to export. Select All Tasks, then Save Configuration to a File:

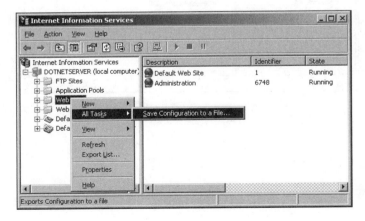

The dialog that appears allows you to enter a file name, and select a folder for the file. As with the backup option we saw earlier, you can encrypt the session keys and "secure" properties with a password:

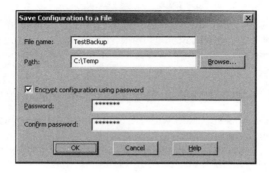

Restoring the Configuration from a File

The saved configuration files can be used to create or restore the corresponding subset(s) of the IIS configuration, by importing all or part of them. In the previous section of this chapter, we saved the complete subset of Web Sites as a file named TestBackup file. To restore this, right-click on the corresponding section to restore into, select New, then Web Site (from file):

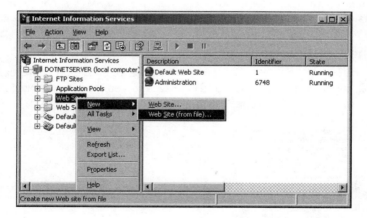

This opens the Import Configuration dialog:

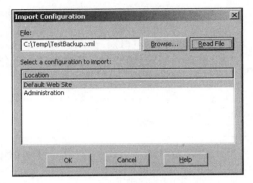

Use the Browse button to select the file, or type the full path and file name, and then click Read File. The content of the file, in terms of the individual object configurations it holds, is displayed in the lower window. Select the site you want to import (you can only select one at a time in the lower window) and click OK. If a site with this name already exists, a dialog asks whether you want to replace the existing one or create a new site with the same name:

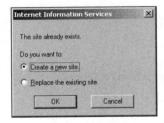

If the saved configuration is encrypted, you'll be prompted for the password to decrypt it before it is imported. Also, note that if you choose to create a new site with the same name, it is installed, but not started. This is because it contains property values that are not permitted. For example, it will respond to the same IP address as the existing site (or may be set to "All Unassigned"). It will also have the same paths configured for virtual and web directories as the original site. However, you can reconfigure these properties, and change the site name in the main IIS Manager window after importing it.

Programmatic Configuration Export and Import

As with backing up and restoring the configuration, IIS includes a script that can be used to programmatically accomplish exactly the same results. The script named iiscnfg.vbs can be used to export the configuration of the complete server, or a subset, to a file. It can also be used to import individual objects (keys) from this file in the same way as the New | Web Site (from file) menu command in IIS Manager that we saw in the previous section.

Saving the Configuration as a file

The general syntax for the `iiscnfg.vbs` script when saving configurations to a file is:

```
iiscnfg /export [/s computer] /f [file-path\]backup-name /sp source-
path [/e encrypt-password] [/children] [/inherited] [/u [domain\]user-
name /p password]
```

The parameters for the `iiscnfg.vbs` script when used for saving configuration data are shown in the following table:

Parameter	Example	Description
/s computer	/s dotnetserver	The name or the IP address of the computer to save the configuration from. If omitted, the default is the local computer.
/f file-path-and-name	/f c:\temp\exported.xml	The file name (and optionally, the path) of the file that will store the configuration. Required parameter.
/sp source-path	/sp /lm/w3svc/1	The LDAP-style path or location key for the object to be saved, as shown in the Location attribute of the object in the MetaBase.xml file. Must be enclosed in double quotes if the path contains any spaces. Required parameter.
/e encrypt-password	/e secret	The password to be used to encrypt the session keys and "secure" values in the exported file.
/children		Include all sub-keys (child objects) of the current object in the file.

Parameter	Example	Description
/inherited		Include any keys from objects higher in the hierarchy that are inherited by this object. Usually required when the configuration data is used to generate a new object on a different server.
/u domain\user	/u mydomain\admin	The user name to run the script under. Can include the domain if required. The account specified must have administrative privileges on the machine.
/p password	/p letmein	The password for the account used to run the script. If omitted, the script prompts for the password when it runs.

As an example, the following screenshot shows the result of executing the command:

As you can see in the previous screen, this creates the file exported.xml, containing the configuration of the Default Web Site as specified by the location path /lm/w3svc/1. This includes all the child objects within the site (such as virtual directories and web directories) because the /children parameter is specified. You can see the Connecting to server message, and the confirmation that the process was completed successfully.

Restoring the Configuration from a File

The general syntax for the iiscnfg.vbs script when importing configurations from a file is:

```
iiscnfg /import [/s computer] /f [file-path\]backup-name /sp source-
path /dp destination-path [/e encrypt-password] [/children]
[/inherited] [/merge] [/u [domain\]user-name /p password]
```

123

The parameters for the `iisback.vbs` script used for importing configuration data are shown in the following table:

Parameter	Example	Description
`/s computer`	`/s dotnetserver`	The name or the IP address of the computer to import the configuration to. If omitted, the default is the local computer.
`/f file-path-and-name`	`/f c:\temp\exported.xml`	The file name (and optionally the path) of the file that holds the saved configuration data. Required parameter.
`/sp source-path`	`/sp /lm/w3svc/1`	The LDAP-style path or location key for the object to be imported from the saved configuration file, as shown in the `Location` attribute of the object in the `MetaBase.xml` file. Must be enclosed in double quotes if the path contains any spaces. Required parameter.
`/dp destination-path`	`/dp /lm/w3svc/2`	The LDAP-style path or location key for the object after it has been imported. Must be enclosed in double quotes if the path contains any spaces. Required parameter.
`/e encrypt-password`	`/e secret`	The password to be used to decrypt the session keys and "secure" values as they are imported.

Parameter	Example	Description
/children		Import all sub-keys (child objects) of the current object from the file.
/inherited		Import any keys for objects higher in the hierarchy that are inherited by this object. Usually required when the configuration data is used to generate a new object on a different server.
/merge		Specifies that only keys that exist in the XML file and not in the current metabase should be imported and added to the current configuration. Without this parameter, all the keys in the XML file are imported, over-writing any with the same location name in the current metabase.
/u domain\user	/u mydomain\admin	The user name to run the script under. Can include the domain if required. The account specified must have administrative privileges on the machine.
/p password	/p letmein	The password for the account used to run the script. If omitted, the script prompts for the password when it runs.

As an example, the following screenshot shows the result of executing the command:

```
C:\WINDOWS\system32\cmd.exe                                    _□×
C:\>iiscnfg /import /f c:\temp\exported.xml /sp /lm/w3svc/1 /dp /lm/w3svc/5 /chi
ldren
Connecting to server ...Done.
C:\>_
```

This imports the key /lm/w3svc/1 from the file exported.xml, and also all the child
objects, which between them contain the complete configuration of the Default Web Site
and it's virtual and web directories. The site is imported to the location /lm/w3svc/2.
You can see the Connecting to server message, and the confirmation that the process was
completed successfully.

After the process is completed, the site is visible in IIS Manager, but is stopped. As
before, some of the properties conflict with the existing Default Web Site, but these can
be edited to allow the new site to run. Of course, if the site you are importing does not
already exist on the target machine, it can be imported without conflicting with an
existing site. This suggests that the scripted export and import feature is best suited to:

❑   Copying sites to another unconfigured IIS server, perhaps when populating
    a **web farm**

❑   Making backups of sites that will be used if the original site is corrupted,
    removed or damaged

❑   Creating sites within application setup programs, using the /merge option
    to only add new keys

Managing Applications and Web Extensions

Unlike the previous versions of IIS, IIS 6.0 comes with the "lock down" approach. IIS 6
can only support HTML documents. If you want IIS 6.0 to support ASP or ASP.NET
pages then you have to enable these web extensions for the web applications. This is
the only way IIS 6 can support ASP or ASP.NET applications. This approach provides
maximum security for IIS 6 and hackers can't take advantage of unused features in IIS
6.0. In this section we'll see how to handle applications and web extensions.

We can use the IISExt script to manage all the applications and web extensions. For
example, if you want to list all the applications you can use the /ListApp switch with
IISExt script.

```
C:>IISExt /ListApp
Connecting to server ...Done.
Active Server Pages
Internet Data Connector
Server Side Includes
WebDAV
FrontPage Server Extensions
ASP.NET v1.0.3705
Remote Administration Tool
```

To enable an application you can use the /EnApp switch with IISExt script:

```
C:>IISExt /EnApp "ASP.NET v1.0.3705"
Connecting to server ...Done.
Enabling application complete.
```

To list all the web service extensions we can use the /ListExt switch:

```
C:>IISExt /ListExt
Connecting to server ...Done.
ASP
HTTPODBC
SSINC
WEBDAV
FPSE2002
ASP.NET V1.0.3705
PBS
```

We can also list all the web services extension file names using the /ListFile switch (the previous command shows their names):

```
C:>IISExt /ListFile
Connecting to server ...Done.
C:\Windows\System32\Inetsrv\Asp.dll
C:\Windows\System32\Inetsrv\HTTPODBC.dll
C:\Windows\System32\Inetsrv\SSINC.dll
C:\Windows\System32\Inetsrv\HttpExt.dll
C:\Program Files\Common Files\Microsoft Shared\Web Server
Extensions\50\isapi\_vti_aut\Author.dll
C:\Program Files\Common Files\Microsoft Shared\Web Server
Extensions\50\isapi\_vti_adm\Admin.dll
C:\Program Files\Common Files\Microsoft Shared\Web Server
Extensions\50\isapi\_vti_adm\fpadmdll.dll
C:\Program Files\Common Files\Microsoft Shared\Web Server
Extensions\50\isapi\shtml.dll
C:\Program Files\Common Files\Microsoft Shared\Web Server
Extensions\50\isapi\owssvr.dll
C:\Program Files\Common Files\Microsoft Shared\Web Server
Extensions\50\isapi\fpcount.exe
C:\Windows\Microsoft.NET\Framework\v1.0.3705\aspnet_isapi.dll
C:\Program Files\Phone Book Service\bin\pbserver.dll
```

In the same way we can add, remove and enable web server extensions and files.

Copy Configuration

We've seen so many options to save the configuration information. Most of the options work fine if you are working with one server. What if you want to copy the configuration information from one server to another server? How would you do this? You can't simple export the configuration information from one server to another since the configuration information includes some server specific information that will not make any sense to the destination server. The best way to handle this situation is to use the /Copy switch with the IISCnfg script.

In the following example, we're coping all the configuration information from the current server to the WinDotNetSrv007:

```
C:\> IISCnfg /Copy /ts WinDotNetSrv007 /tu WinDotNetSrv007\_007Admin
/tp !AmAzOn@007

Microsoft (R) Windows Script Host Version 5.6
Copyright (C) Microsoft Corporation 1996-2001. All rights reserved.

Backing up server 127.0.0.1
cmd /c iisback /backup /b iisreplback /overwrite
Backup complete.
Mapping local drive Y: to admin share on server 127.0.0.1
Mapping local drive Z: to admin share on server WinDotNetSrv007
Copying backup files...
cmd /c copy /Y Y:\system32\inetsrv\metaback\iisreplback.*
Z:\system32\inetsrv\metaback
Unmapping local drive Y:
Restoring on server WinDotNetSrv007
cmd /c iisback /restore /s WinDotNetSrv007 /u
WinDotNetSrv007\_007Admin /p !AmAzOn@007 /b iisreplback
Restore complete.
Unmapping local drive Z:
```

If you look at the above results from the script you pretty much understand what's happening. The /Copy switch simply backs up the configuration information from the current server using the /Backup switch. Then it maps drive in the local server with the destination server share. Then it copies the backup files (iisreplback.*) into the destination server. Then it uses the /Restore switch to restore the configuration settings and un-maps all the drives. But when it restores the settings it'll not copy the server specific information such as files inside the web sites and FTP sites.

> When you copy the configuration settings from one server to another, the physical file or folder path defined in one server may not be correct on the destination server. Make sure you edit this information.

If you remember the utility that was shipped with the previous IIS version IISSync.Exe, it is being replaced with the /Copy switch.

Save Configuration to Disk

When you make a change to the IIS configuration using the MMC the information is first written to memory. Then it is written to the XML file using the scheduled update, which could be several minutes later. So, if you open the configuration file right after the MMC change you may not see the changes in the XML file. One way to force the changes to the XML file is to use the /Save switch with the IISCnfg script.

```
C:>IISCnfg /Save
Connecting to server ... Done.
Metadata successfully flushed to disk.
```

Programmatic Administration

If you come from a UNIX or Linux background, you would be familiar with script-based administration. Script-based administration makes a lot of sense when managing multiple servers. IIS 6.0 offers tools that enable you to administer services using scripts or applications. IIS 6.0 allows four ways to administer from code:

❑ Command line scripts

❑ IIS 6.0 Windows Management Instrumentation (or WMI) provider

❑ IIS 6.0 Active Directory Service Interface (or ADSI) provider

❑ Admin Base Objects (Or ABO)

The command line scripts that we used previously can also be used inside another script to make things work for you. Within all the available options, this is going to be the easiest option since there is no need to learn any object model. All we need to do is to know how to use these scripts and we're good to go.

The Admin Base Objects provide low-level access to the IIS Object Model for C++ programmers. Using ABO C++ and Visual C++, programmers can write some sophisticated applications. As a matter of fact, IIS reads the Metabase.Xml into memory using ABO. Since ABO can't be used in scripts, we cannot use it to investigate ABO since they'll not be handy for us to do stuff quickly. In this section, we'll learn how to script IIS Administration Objects using both WMI and ADSI.

Using WMI

Web-Based Enterprise System Management Architecture (**WBEM**) is an open standard specification defined by the independent organization called **Desktop Management Task Force** (DMTF http://www.dmtf.org/standards/standard_dmi.php). WEBM is an industry standard to manage physical and logical resources such as computers, networks, etc. The WEBM architecture is based on **Common Information Model** (**CIM**). CIM is a unified standard way of defining the physical and logical objects via a schema. The WEBM architecture is object-oriented in nature. Windows Management Instrument (WMI) is Microsoft's answer to WEBM and almost all the objects and collections follow CIM standards.

WMI gives the developers enormous power over all the physical and logical components available in the system, including from operating system to Network, to Processes, to Printers, to IIS. This gives us control over these elements and we're able to build a web-based management tool or use a script, which makes the maintenance easier.

Why WMI?

We can achieve most of the functionality available with WMI by using Win32 API calls or using proprietary interfaces provided by the service:

❑   Most of the time proprietary interfaces like Win32 API calls are hard to use and they can't be used from every development environment. For example, we can't use Win32 API calls from ASP. On the other hand, if we can wrap the Win32 API call in a COM component it is very easy for us to access the information using a script from all the development environments including ASP, .NET, Windows Scripting Host, etc.

❑   When we're dealing with hardware-based resource management, we have a wide variety of hardware vendors, servers, and services, and we have to understand each vendor' specific APIs to manipulate the hardware. For example, if you want to find the CISCO hardware performance information, you have to understand their APIs and write programs to read the information from the hardware device. This will become a very tedious process when it involves multiple vendors. On the other hand, if we work with WMI we must understand only one set of classes and collections and we'll be able to access any hardware information exposed by WMI.

WMI is an integral part of Windows Server 2003 operating system. It is also available for Windows NT 4.0 and Windows 95/98. WMI consist of two major components. One is the actual WMI component (WINMGMT.EXE) and the CIM repository. WINMGMT.EXE runs as a service on NT/Windows 2000/2003 OS and runs as a standalone EXE on 95/98 OS. The CIM repository is the central database that stores all the manageable static data. The following diagram shows the architecture of WMI:

Figure 1

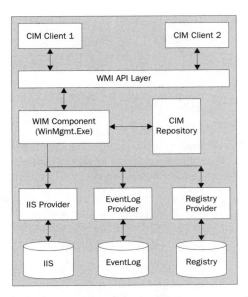

When client applications request WMI data, those calls are passed through
`WINMGMT.EXE`. If the requested information is static, then the static information will be
fetched from the CIM Repository (CIM Repository is stored in a single file at
`\winnt\system32\webm\repository`) and sent back to the client applications. If
the requested information is dynamic then `WINMGMT` calls the specific WMI provider
passes the call, and returns the results to the client applications. For example, when we
try to query information from IIS or Windows Registry, WMI uses the appropriate
provider to get the information for us.

Basic Objects

WMI consist of few basic classes that make up the whole interface. If you are familiar
with the classes then you can easily program against WMI. The following figure shows
the relationship between these objects:

Figure 2

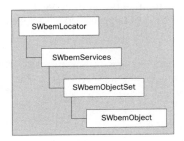

The following table discusses the objects in more detail:

CIM Class	Description
SWbemLocator	This is the topmost object in the WMI hierarchy. We can use the ConnectServer method of the SWbemLocator object to establish a connection to WMI (either local machine or remote machine).
SWbemServices	We can use the SWbemServices object to perform any operation against a namespace. ConnectServer method of the SWbemLocator object returns an instance of SWbemServices object.
SWbemObjectSet	SWbemObjectSet object is a collection that holds individual SWbemObject objects. InstancesOf method of SWbemServices object returns the SWbemObjectSet object.
SWbemObject	This object gives an instance of single CIM class.
SWbemSink	This object is used to perform asynchronous operations with the WMI data.

The SWbemLocator object establishes the service with the WMI provider and returns a SWbemServices object. Using the SWbemServices object we can get a collection of SWbemObjectSet or a single instance of SWbemObject and work on the object.

The next big advantage of WMI is its query and association support. The WMI query supports a subset of SQL to access WMI data. WMI borrows some of the SQL functionality as WMI Query Language (WQL). Since WMI is truly object-oriented, objects and properties are associated outside the boundaries of a containment model. Therefore the association allows selections and modifications of object and properties containment boundaries. All the classes of a provider are contained in a namespace. For example, the MicrosoftIISv2 namespace contains all the other namespaces like the one for IIS.

The SWbemLocator object exposes the ConnectServer method that allows us to connect to a destination server. While connecting to the server using the ConnectServer method we can specify parameters such as server name, namespace (for example, "root/MicrosoftIISv2" is the namespace for the IIS 6.0 server), username, password, etc.

The SWbemServices object exposes few important methods and properties that allow us to get WMI object collections or single WMI object. The following table lists a few important members of the SWbemServices object:

Member	Description
AssociatorsOf	Returns a collection of objects that are associated with a specified WMI object. For example, if you want to get a collection of virtual directories within a web site you can use this method to get the virtual directories collection.
ExecMethod	Executes an object's method. For example, if you want to start a web site then you have to get the instance of the site and use ExecMethod to start the site.
ExecQuery	Executes a query to retrieve a collection of objects which is equivalent to the AssociatorsOf method.
Get	Retrieves an instance of an object.
InstancesOf	Retrieves a collection of instances of a specified class.

These methods are also available in asynchronous flavor; you add the Async keyword at the end of all the members. For example, InstancesOfAsync is the asynchronous flavor of the InstancesOf method.

The SWbemServices object is a collection and each item of collection will return an instance of the SWbemObject object. The SWbemServices object can be retrieved by using AssociatorsOf, InstancesOf, and ExecQuery methods of the SWbemServices object. The SWbemObject object includes dynamic properties supported by the object that we're querying.

So far, we've seen WMI concepts including classes and objects. Let's now see what it takes to connect to the IIS 6.0 WMI provider.

The WMI object model is easily accessible, like ADO, where you can open a recordset object without opening an ADO connection object explicitly.

Let us look at the VB Script code (ListWeb.Vbs) which lists all the web sites in a given server. All the logic resides in the VBScript function ListWebSites and we call the function with the computer name:

```
Call ListWebSites("DOTNETSERVER")

Function ListWebSites (sComputer)
    WScript.Echo " "
    WScript.Echo "Web Sites on the server " + sComputer
    WScript.Echo "_____"
    WScript.Echo " "

    Dim locatorObj, providerObj , nodeObj
```

```
      Set locatorObj = CreateObject("WbemScripting.SWbemLocator")
      Set providerObj = locatorObj.ConnectServer(sComputer, _
                              "root/MicrosoftIISv2")

      Set nodeObj = providerObj.InstancesOf("IIsWebServerSetting")

      'Loop through the sites collection
      For Each instSite in nodeObj
      WScript.Echo " " & instSite.Name & " - " & _
              instSite.ServerComment
      Next

      WScript.Echo " "
      WScript.Echo "_____"

      Set locatorObj = Nothing
      Set providerObj = Nothing
      Set nodeObj = Nothing

      WScript.Quit
End Function
```

Here is the output that shows the metabase ID of the web site and the name of it. The web site information is from the IIsWebServerSettings WMI class:

In the same way we can list all the FTP sites on the given server. Here is the code for that:

```
Call ListFtpSites("DOTNETSERVER")

Function ListFtpSites (sComputer)
...
...
    Set locatorObj = CreateObject("WbemScripting.SWbemLocator")
    Set providerObj = locatorObj.ConnectServer(sComputer,
                    "root/MicrosoftIISv2")

    Set nodeObj = providerObj.InstancesOf("IIsFtpServerSetting")

...
...
End Function
```

The only change in the code is that we've changed the caption and we're getting all the FTP site names from the `IIsFtpServerSettings` class:

The remaining code stays the same. In the same way we can also query all the SMTP and NNTP sites by changing the class from `IIsFtpServerSettings` to `IIsSmtpServerSettings` and `IIsNntpServerSettings`.

Let's see how we can list all the virtual directories under a web site or FTP site. The virtual directory information is not stored as a collection in the web site object. Instead it is stored in the `IIsDirectory` object with the special attribute (`IIsWebVirtualDir`). So we've to associate the `IIsDirectory` object with its attribute to get the collection. Here is the implementation:

```
Call ListWebVDir("DOTNETSERVER", "745575007")

Function ListWebVDir(sComputer, SiteID)
    WScript.Echo " "
    WScript.Echo "Virtual directories on the site " + SiteID
    WScript.Echo "_____"
    WScript.Echo " "

    Dim locatorObj, providerObj, nodeObj, strQuery

    Set locatorObj = CreateObject("WbemScripting.SWbemLocator")
    Set providerObj = locatorObj.ConnectServer(sComputer, _
                                    "root/MicrosoftIISv2")
    strQuery = "ASSOCIATORS OF {IIsDirectory='W3SVC/" & SiteID & _
            "/Root'} WHERE ResultClass = IIsWebVirtualDir "

    Set nodeObj = providerObj.ExecQuery(strQuery)

    For each Obj in nodeObj
        WScript.Echo " " & Obj.Name
    Next

    WScript.Echo " "
    WScript.Echo "_____"

    Set locatorObj = Nothing
    Set providerObj = Nothing
```

135

```
        Set nodeObj = Nothing
        Set strQuery = Nothing

        WScript.Quit
End Function
```

What we've done here is queried all the web site for the given metabase ID and we've enumerated the returned collection.

We can modify the above code a little bit to work with FTP virtual directories. Here is the implementation:

```
Call ListFtpVDir("DOTNETSERVER", "1")

Function ListFtpVDir(sComputer, SiteID)
....
....
....
    Set locatorObj = CreateObject("WbemScripting.SWbemLocator")
    Set providerObj = locatorObj.ConnectServer(sComputer, _
                            "root/MicrosoftIISv2")
```
```
strQuery = "ASSOCIATORS OF {IIsDirectory='MSFTPSVC/" & SiteID & _
            "/Root'} WHERE ResultClass = IIsFtpVirtualDir"
....
End Function
```

The screenshot below shows both of these scripts in action:

The entire code for all the scripts are available for download from http://www.wrox.com/.

The only change is the query statement, which filters all the FTP virtual directories. Let's see how we can create virtual directories for both web and FTP sites. Here is the code snippet that creates a web virtual directory. This function takes four parameters; first the computer name, followed by the metabase ID, the virtual directory name and the path.

```
Call CreateWebVDir("DOTNETSERVER", "1", "Test1", "D:\Test")

Function CreateWebVDir (sComputer, SiteID, VirName, VirDirPath)
   WScript.Echo " "
   WScript.Echo "Creating a new virtual directory ..."
   WScript.Echo " "

   Dim locatorObj, providerObj , nodeObj, VDirobj

   Set locatorObj = CreateObject("WbemScripting.SWbemLocator")
   Set providerObj = locatorObj.ConnectServer(sComputer, _
                     "root/MicrosoftIISv2")
```

As usual, we've connected to the IIS 6.0 namespace in the specified computer.

```
   Set nodeObj = providerObj.Get("IIsWebVirtualDirSetting")
```

Then we've received an instance of the class IIsWebVirtualDirSetting, which will allow us to create a new virtual directory. Since all the WMI objects are independent of each other, we're calling the method SpawnInstance_() of the IIsWebVirtualDirSetting class to create virtual directory properties.

```
   'Get the properties of the Virtual dir
   Set VDirobj = nodeObj.SpawnInstance_()
   VDirobj.Name = "W3SVC/" & SiteID & "/Root/" & VirName
   VDirobj.Path = VirDirPath

   ' Set web virtual directory properties
   VDirobj.AuthFlags = 5 ' AuthNTLM + AuthAnonymous
   VDirobj.EnableDefaultDoc = True
   VDirobj.AccessFlags = 513 ' read, script
   VDirobj.Put_()
```

Then we assign values to the properties and call the Put_() method to save the information. We assign an application pool to the virtual directory and give it a friendly name:

```
   'Create a Pooled application on ROOT WebVDir
   Set VDirobj = providerObj.Get("IIsWebVirtualDir='W3SVC/" & SiteID & _
   "/Root/" & VirName & "'")
   VDirobj.AppCreate2(2)

   'Update AppFriendlyName property
   Set VDirobj = providerObj.Get("IIsWebVirtualDirSetting='W3SVC/" & _
   SiteID & "/Root/" & VirName & "'")
   VDirobj.AppFriendlyName = VirName
   VDirobj.Put_()
```

```
        Set locatorObj = Nothing
        Set providerObj = Nothing
        Set nodeObj = Nothing
        Set VDirobj = Nothing

        WScript.Quit
End Function
```

In the same way we can create a FTP virtual directory:

```
Call CreateFtpVDir("DOTNETSERVER", "1", "Test1", "D:\Test")

Function CreateFtpVDir (sComputer, SiteID, VirName, VirDirPath)
    ...
    ...
    ...
    Set locatorObj = CreateObject("WbemScripting.SWbemLocator")
    Set providerObj = locatorObj.ConnectServer(sComputer, _
                    "root/MicrosoftIISv2")
    Set nodeObj = providerObj.get("IIsFtpVirtualDirSetting")

    ...
End Function
```

The only change is the virtual directory class name and we don't have the extra properties and the application pool information. Other than that, both the codes are identical.

Let's see how we can delete a virtual directory of web and FTP sites. To delete a virtual directory we get the instance of the site. Then we delete all the applications recursively that are stored in the virtual directory. Then we delete the virtual directory. The following code does the same:

```
Call DeleteWebVDir("DOTNETSERVER", "1", "Test")

Function DeleteWebVDir (sComputer, SiteID, VirName)
    WScript.Echo " "
    WScript.Echo "Deleting virtual directory ..."
    WScript.Echo " "

    Dim locatorObj, providerObj , nodeObj

    Set locatorObj = CreateObject("WbemScripting.SWbemLocator")
    Set providerObj = locatorObj.ConnectServer(sComputer, _
                                    "root/MicrosoftIISv2")
    Set nodeObj = providerObj.Get("IIsWebVirtualDir='W3SVC/" & SiteID & _
                            "/Root/" & VirName & "'")

    'Delete application recursively in this virtual dir
     nodeObj.AppDelete(True)
```

```
      'Delete Virtual Directory
      nodeObj.Delete_()
      if (Err<>0) then
          WScript.Echo "Oops An Error Occured! Can't Delete the" & _
                      "virtual directory"
      Else
          WScript.Echo "Virtual directory " & VirName & "    successfully
      deleted..."
      End if

      Set locatorObj = Nothing
      Set providerObj = Nothing
      Set nodeObj = Nothing

      WScript.Quit
End Function
```

Here is the FTP implementation of the code. The only difference is that, we don't have to delete all the applications recursively.

```
Call DeleteFtpVDir("DOTNETSERVER", "1", "Test")

Function DeleteFtpVDir (sComputer, SiteID, VirName)
...
...

    Set locatorObj = CreateObject("WbemScripting.SWbemLocator")
    Set providerObj = locatorObj.ConnectServer(sComputer,
                      "root/MicrosoftIISv2")
    Set nodeObj = providerObj.Get("IIsFtpVirtualDir='MSFTPSVC/" & _
                  SiteID _& "/Root/" & VirName & "'")
...
...
End Function
```

Using ADSI

Active Directory Service Interface (ADSI) is a set of open interfaces that abstracts the capabilities of directory services from different network providers to present a single view for accessing and managing network resources. Administrators and developers can use ADSI services to enumerate and manage resources in a directory service, no matter which network environment contains the resource. This includes **LDAP (Lightweight Directory Access Protocol)** and **NDS (Novell Directory Services)** based directory. Many of the Microsoft products support an LDAP protocol-based directory for administration including IIS. However, IIS supports LDAP and we can use ADSI to access IIS objects.

Active Directory Service Interface (ADSI) provides straightforward standard syntax for accessing any directory services object including IIS Admin Objects. All the IIS objects are accessed through the `IIS://` ADSI format. The rest of the information can be the path that we're trying to access. For example, "`IIS://Sruthi-Anusri/W3SVC/1/Root`" path will return the instance of my Default Web Site. In this section we'll see how to access the IIS Admin object through ADSI provider. We'll rewrite all WMI samples with ADSI.

Let's start with a list of all the web sites in a given computer. What the code does is very simple. We're getting an instance of web server and we're looping through a collection and only listing the web sites:

```
Call ListWebSites("DOTNETSERVER")

Function ListWebSites (sComputer)
    WScript.Echo " "
    WScript.Echo "Web Sites on the server " + sComputer
    WScript.Echo "_____"
    WScript.Echo " "

    Dim WebServerRootObj

    Set WebServerRootObj = GetObject("IIS://" & sComputer & _
                        "/W3SVC")
    For each Obj in WebServerRootObj
    'The web server will return all the root objects
    'we're filtering only the web sites using the following statement
    If IsNumeric(Obj.Name) Then
        WScript.Echo " " & Obj.Name & " - " & Obj.ServerComment
    End if
    Next

    WScript.Echo " "
    WScript.Echo "_____"

    Set WebServerRootObj = Nothing

    WScript.Quit
End Function
```

Here in the same way we can also list all the FTP sites with very minimal code change. Instead of getting the instance of web server, we're getting an instance of FTP service. The remaining code stays the same:

```
Call ListFtpSites("DOTNETSERVER")

Function LisFtptSites (sComputer)
...
..
```

```
..
   'Open the object for the first virtual web server root
   Set WebServerRootObj = GetObject("IIS://" & sComputer &
                             "/MSFTPSVC")
...
..
...
End Function
```

Again by simply changing the ADSI path we can also read NNTP and SMTP services:

```
Set WebServerRootObj = GetObject("IIS://" & sComputer & "/NNTPSVC")
Set WebServerRootObj = GetObject("IIS://" & sComputer & "/SMTPSVC")
```

Let's look at the code that lists all the virtual directories in a given web or FTP site.

```
Call ListWebVDir("DOTNETSERVER", "1")

Function ListWebVDir(sComputer, SiteID)
   WScript.Echo " "
   WScript.Echo "Virtual directories on the site " + SiteID
   WScript.Echo "_____"
   WScript.Echo " "

   Dim WebServerRootObj

   Set WebVdirObj = GetObject("IIS://" & sComputer & "/W3SVC/" & _
               SiteID & "/Root")
   WScript.Echo " " & WebVdirObj.Name

   For each Obj in WebVdirObj
      WScript.Echo " " & Obj.Name
   Next

   WScript.Echo " "
   WScript.Echo "_____"

   Set WebVdirObj = Nothing

   WScript.Quit
End Function
```

By changing the following line we can list all the FTP virtual directories.

```
Set WebVdirObj = GetObject("IIS://" & sComputer & "/MSFTPSVC/" & _
SiteID & "/Root")
```

Creating virtual directories is also very straightforward. We get the instance of the web or FTP root. Then we call the `Create` method with the virtual directory name. After that we call the `SetInfo` method to save the changes. Then we set necessary properties with the default values and call the `SetInfo` method to save the changes again:

```
Call CreateWebVDir("DOTNETSERVER", "1", "Test", "D:\Test")

Function CreateWebVDir (sComputer, SiteID, VirName, VirDirPath)
    WScript.Echo " "
    WScript.Echo "Creating a new virtual directory ..."
    WScript.Echo " "

    Dim WebSiteObj

    'Open the object for the first virtual web server root
    Set WebSiteObj = GetObject("IIS://" & sComputer & "/W3SVC/" & _
                    SiteID & "/Root")

    if (Err <>0) then
        WScript.Echo "Oops An Error Occured! Can't access the web site "
    Else
    'Create the virtual directory
    Dim VdirObj
    Set VdirObj = WebSiteObj.Create("IIsWebVirtualDir", VirName)
    VdirObj.SetInfo

    if (Err<>0) then
    WScript.Echo "Oops An Error Occurred! Can't create virtual" & _
                "directory"
    Else
    'Set the permissions to read, script, and directory browsing
    VdirObj.AccessRead = True
    VdirObj.AccessScript = True
    VdirObj.EnableDirBrowsing = True
    VdirObj.Put "Path", (VirDirPath)

    'Save the information
     VdirObj.SetInfo
    if (Err<> 0) then
    WScript.Echo "Oops An Error Occurred! Unable to save the virtual
                directory information. Please check the path."
    else
    WScript.Echo "Virtual directory " & VditName & _
                "successfully created..."
    end if
    end if

    Set VdirObj = Nothing
      end if

    Set WebSiteObj = Nothing
    WScript.Quit
End Function
```

With minimal changes we can make the above code work with FTP sites:

```
Call CreateFtpVDir("DOTNETSERVER", "1", "Test", "D:\Test")

Function CreateFtpVDir (sComputer, SiteID, VirName, VirDirPath)
...
...

    Dim WebSiteObj

    'Open the object for the first virtual web server root
    Set WebSiteObj = GetObject("IIS://" & sComputer & "/MSFTPSVC/" &
                                SiteID _ & "/Root")

    if (Err <>0) then
        WScript.Echo "Oops An Error Occured! Can't access the web site "
    Else
    'Create the virtual directory
    Dim VdirObj
      Set VdirObj = WebSiteObj.Create("IIsFTPVirtualDir", VirName)
      VdirObj.SetInfo
    if (Err<>0) then
        WScript.Echo "Oops An Error Occured! Can't create virtual
                      directory"
    Else
        VdirObj.Put "Path", (VirDirPath)
...
...

    End Function
```

To delete a virtual directory all we do is get the instance of the virtual directory and call the `Delete` method. Here is the code sample:

```
Call DeleteWebVDir("DOTNETSERVER", "1", "Test")

Function DeleteWebVDir (sComputer, SiteID, VirName)
    WScript.Echo " "
    WScript.Echo "Deleting virtual directory ..."
    WScript.Echo " "

    Dim WebSiteObj
    'Open the object for the first virtual web server root
    Set WebSiteObj = GetObject("IIS://" & sComputer & "/W3SVC/" & _
    SiteID & "/Root")

    If (Err <> 0) then
        WScript.Echo "Oops An Error Occured! Can't access the web site "
    Else
    'Delete Virtual Directory
     WebSiteObj.Delete "IIsObject",VirName
```

```
if (Err<>0) then
    WScript.Echo "Oops An Error Occured! Can't Delete the virtual" & _
              "directory"
Else
    WScript.Echo "Virtual directory " & VirName &
              " successfully deleted..."
end if
End if

Set WebSiteObj = Nothing
WScript.Quit

End Function
```

This simple change will make the code work with the FTP virtual directory.

```
'Open the object for the first virtual web server root
Set WebSiteObj = GetObject("IIS://" & sComputer & "/MSFTPSVC/" & _
SiteID & "/Root")
```

Remote Administration

Administrating an IIS server remotely is always a challenge since accessing the server outside the firewall always poses a lot of problems. In this section, we'll see the ways in which we can administrate an IIS server and the pros and cons of it.

IIS MMC

We'll start our quest with IIS MMC. If you right-click on the root node of IIS, you'll see an option to connect to a different computer:

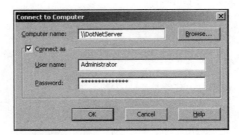

The main problem with this option is that MMC uses **Remote Procedure Calls (RPC)** to connect and manage the other server. The RPC calls use NetBIOS over TCP/IP on port 139. This is the single most dangerous port on the Internet. All "File and Printer Sharing" (including MMC RPC) calls on a Windows machine run on this port. This is the first port hackers want to connect to, and the port that firewalls block. Of course this option is viable if you are administrating the servers within the firewall. However, this is not a good option since opening port 139 lead to security implications for our network.

Using Telnet

Telnet is a command prompt-only option that can be used to administrate IIS 6.0. Since IIS 6.0 comes with many command line administration scripts this option is very attractive. The problem is that, Telnet works on port 23 and we have to open the port on the first wall, if you are administrating outside the firewall. There are many problems with opening this port including a few buffer overflow issues associated with Telnet services and these can be triggered through large username, password or terminal type options. Again this varies from OS to OS.

Moreover, the way Telnet handles the password is not very safe. For example a typical Telnet URL will look like:

```
telnet://user:password@host:port
OR
telnet://ssivakumar@MyPassword@WinDotNetSrv007:23
```

As you can see, the password is right there in the URL. Imagine sending an administration account name and password over an unsecure wire to connect to the telnet service. You can however, use third-party add-ons that secure the Telnet session.

Windows Terminal Services

The next popular option is to use **Windows Terminal Services** (**WTS**). The WTS uses Microsoft's proprietary RDP protocol, which uses TCP port 3389 on the server. This forces us to put a hole in the firewall for the port. You can secure the setup of the WTS with 128-bit MD5 encryption and can't feasibly be broken at this time.

WTS remote administration is a better option than the IIS MMC option because it allows to manage the entire server including checking the configuration files, IIS log files, etc. We can even run the IIS 6.0 command line utilities using WTS. Moreover, WTS works fairly well with low bandwidth connections, and supports 128-bit encryption.

The second advantage with WTS is that, if you install the whole of the bulky WTS components on the client, you can install **Windows Terminal Services Advanced Client** (**WTSAC**), which is an ActiveX control that can be hosted from a supported web browser such as IE. The one thing you've to watch for is to make sure you place the WTSAC files in a secure place and map them as an IIS virtual directory with strict ACLs. Make sure you are using Basic authentication with 128 bit SSL. Since we're accessing the server using an ActiveX control the first authentication will occur on port 80 (if you are using SSL then it'll be port 443). After authentication the server communication will switch port 3389 on the server. If you want to install the WTSAC, go to Control Panel | Add or Remove Programs | Windows Setup | Web Application Server| Internet Information Services (IIS) | World Wide Web Services | Remote Desktop Web Connection. For more information see the Microsoft Support Article at http://support.microsoft.com/default.aspx?scid=KB;EN-US;284931.

Web-Based Remote Administration

Windows Server 2003 includes a plain HTML/JavaScript-based web application that can be used to administer IIS 6.0. Nevertheless, you can administer everything from managing Windows Server 2003 (including web server, web sites, virtual directories, etc), network, users, disks, etc. By considering all the above options, the web-based remote administration option looks very safe.

As we know, IIS 6.0 comes with a fully locked-down option. Therefore, the web-based remote administration application is not installed by default. If you want to install the web tool, you have to go to Start | Control Panel | Add or Remove Programs. In the Add or Remove Programs panel, click on the Add/Remove Windows components button. You will be presented with the Windows Component Wizard. Here, select the Web Application Server option and click on the Details button:

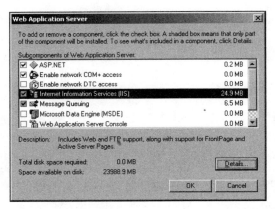

Select the Internet Information Service (IIS) option here and click on the Details button again. In the Internet Information Service(IIS) panel, click on the Details again and click on the Remote Administration(HTML) option :

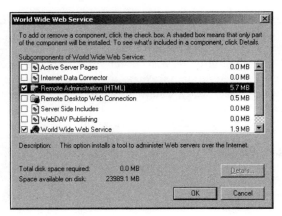

Here is a sample screen shot that shows the list of web sites running on the server:

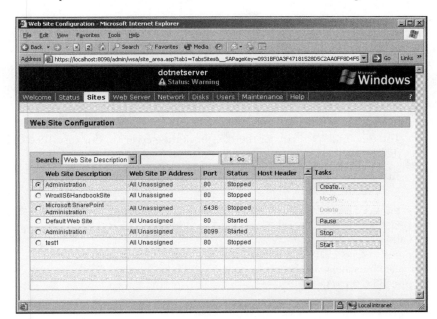

The best way to configure the remote access scenario is
using Virtual Private Network **(Or** VPN**). Combining VPN with
any of the either methods will give better security and less
chance of hacking.**

Configuring Quality of Service

Before getting into how to configure Quality of Service (or QoS), we'll learn what the
term Quality of Service means. QoS is the management of the bandwidth available over
the Internet such that particular types of application can have specified bandwidth and
delivery requirements satisfied. It should be noted that, QoS doesn't provide additional
bandwidth, rather it provides a way to manage existing bandwidth in a more
appropriate way for the use that is being made of it.

So how do we measure the QoS of a network? Well, here are ways in which we can do it.

- **Network availability**
  Defines how much of the network is available for use.

- **Thoughput**
  Defines the amount of data transferred between the server and the client in the given time.

- **Latency**
  The time taken to transfer the data from the server (in our case IIS 6.0) to the client.

- **Jitter**
  Defines the amount of signals destroyed during the network travel.

- **Packet Loss**
  Defines the percentage of packet lost during the network transmission.

When it comes to QoS in IIS 6.0, we can take few steps to configure IIS 6.0 components such as sites, application pools, IIS 6.0 resources, etc. Let's see how we can configure IIS 6.0 for QoS.

Limiting Connections & Bandwidth Throttling

Limiting connection will restrict a number of simultaneous connections to your web site or server. When a number of connections reach the limit that is specified in the configuration, then the client will receive an error message 403.9 Forbidden – Too Many Users. This option ensures a few things:

- This option conserves the bandwidth for other users of the server, if any, such as other web sites, FTP services, NNTP services, SMTP services, etc.

- This option also conserves memory

- Limiting connections is one way to protect against Denial of Service attack (or DoS)

Bandwidth throttling is another way of ensuring that a particular IIS 6.0 service uses a specified number of bandwidths in the available bandwidth pool. When we're configuring the throttling bandwidth option, IIS 6.0 uses the "**Packet Scheduler**" to manage the data packets sent. The options can be configured either for a web site or globally for all the sites. You can configure limiting connections and bandwidth throttling options on the Performance tab of the web site's Properties dialog as for an individual web site.

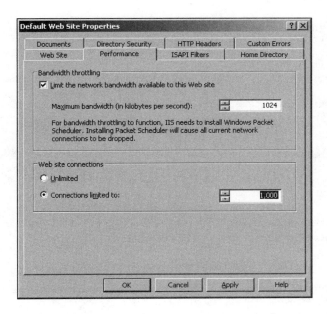

When you configure the bandwidth-throttling option from IIS 6.0 MMC, the Packet Scheduler is automatically installed and the default value is set at 1 MB (1024 bytes per second). If you configure this option programmatically, either using ADSI or WMI, you have to install the Packet Scheduler manually. The next thing to remember is that, the bandwidth throttling value should be always greater than 1024 bytes, since Packet Scheduler can't work with anything below 1024 bytes. The following script is based on ADSI and can change the connection timeout value using script:

```
Call SetConnTimeout("DOTNETSERVER", "1333745956", "Test", 2000)

Function SetConnTimeout (sComputer, SiteID, VirName, ConnTimeout)
   WScript.Echo " "
   WScript.Echo "Setting Connection Timeout value ..."
   WScript.Echo " "

   Dim WebSiteObj
   'Open the object for the first virtual web server root
   Set WebSiteObj = GetObject("IIS://" & sComputer & "/W3SVC/" & _
   SiteID & "/Root")

   If (Err <> 0) then
      WScript.Echo "Oops An Error Occured! Can't access the web site "
   Else

   'Set the value
   WebSiteObj.Put "ConnectionTimeout",VirName
```

```
    'Save the changes
    WebSiteObj.SetInfo

    if (Err<>0) then
        WScript.Echo "Oops An Error Occured! Can't change the value"
    Else
        WScript.Echo "successfully updated the value..."
    end if
    End if

    Set WebSiteObj = Nothing
    WScript.Quit

End Function
```

If you enable the bandwidth throttling using the script, then you can manually install the Pocket Scheduler using the following steps:

❏   Open Network Connections

❏   Go to the Property dialog of the Local Area Connection and select the QoS Packet Scheduler checkbox there

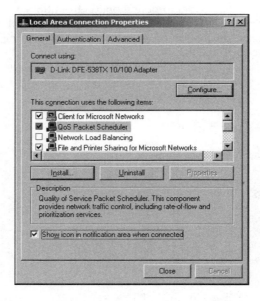

You can also install the QoS Packet Scheduler component by clicking on the Install | Service | Add buttons, and Select QoS Packet Scheduler and click the OK button.

If you have a backup network card on your server then you have to do the same for the backup network card.

Even if you specify the bandwidth throttling value for all the web sites, this will not affect the FTP sites. The only way to change the bandwidth throttling for FTP sites is to use the Services tab on the FTP Sites tree node. One more thing to note here is that a bandwidth throttling value can't be set for individual FTP sites.

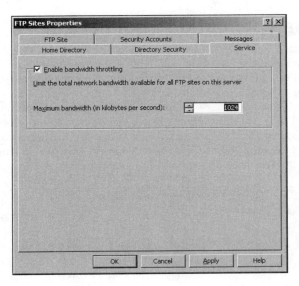

We can also configure the FTP sites for connection limits. Go to the Properties page of the FTP Sites and you'll see a section called "FTP site connections".

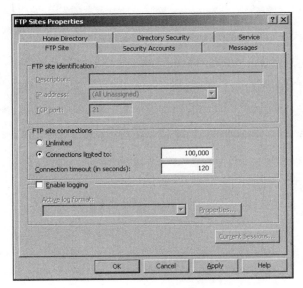

> **Bandwidth throttling is not supported for Internet Protocol Version 6 (or IP V6) web sites.**

Configuring Application Pool Length

When a request reaches the IIS 6.0 server, it is handled by the universal listener. The universal listener reads the application pool length limit parameter and determines how many requests can be queued. If the current request exceeds the configured setting, HTTP error message 503 is sent back to the client. If this number is a larger number and your IIS server's throughput is low, then a lot of requests will be queued on the server and this will overload the server. A better way to handle the problem is by setting the max number for the application pool; otherwise the application pool will queue the requests until the server runs out of memory. This can be configured using Performance tab in the Properties dialog box of the Application Pools tree node.

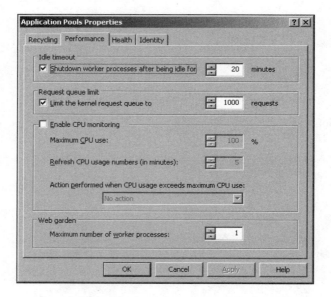

This value can be set globally for all the application pools or for a specific application pool.

Configuring Keep-Alive and Connection Timeout

The HTTP Keep-Alive is an HTTP specification standard that can significantly reduce the stress on the web server. Let's look at the lifetime of a page. Let's say IIS 6.0 is serving an HTML page that has three graphics. If the HTTP Keep-Alive setting is not turned on then, the client has to make four calls to the web server to get the whole page (one call for the HTML page and three calls for three graphics). On the server side, again it's the same story. IIS 6.0 will create four different connections to serve the page back to the client. Moreover, due to the additional number of connections, the server does more processing and uses more resources. On top of that, the browser becomes un-responsive due to the slow connection (high-latency). If we enable the HTTP Keep-Alive option, the same connection will be used to serve all the resources that page includes, which will reduce the stress on the server.

To enable or disable the HTTP Keep-Alive service, go to Web Site tab on the Properties dialog of the Web Site Properties tree node. Then check or uncheck the "Enable HTTP Keep-Alive" checkbox in the Connection section.

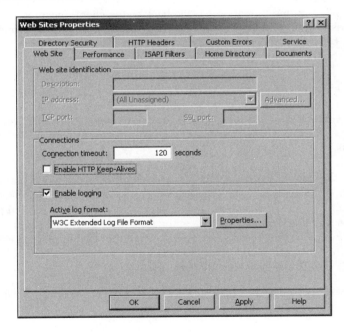

By default HTTP Keep-Alive is enabled during the installation process.

Configuring connection timeouts is another way of reducing stress on the IIS server. When configured, connection timeouts reduce the number of ideal connections and time required to process those ideal connections. The connection timeouts can be categorized as follows:

153

- ❑ The client sends data to server and idly waits for reply. This is connection timeout.

- ❑ The server is waiting idly since the client had connected to the server but didn't submit any data for processing. This is server listen timeout.

- ❑ The minimum number of bytes that can be sent back to the client per second. This is response timeout.

- ❑ The minimum numbers of bytes the server can accept per second, which will preclude clients that connect with unreasonably slow connections. This is request timeout.

When we configure the ConnectionTimeout property in IIS, it enforces all the above types of timeout in conjunction with the MinFileBytesPerSec metabase property. The ConnectionTimeout property specifies the time in minutes that will be used by IIS 6.0 to wait for the inactive connection before terminating it.

The MinFileBytesPerSec property specifies the number of seconds the server should wait while sending the requested file back to the client; meaning the length of time in seconds the server should wait for the transfer to happen between the server and the client before the server closes the connection. The timeout value is always calculated by the following formula:

```
Timeout = (ConnectionTimeout + File Size) / MinFileBytesPerSec
```

The ConnectionTimeout property can be configured using either the IIS MMC or scripts. However the MinFileBytesPerSec metabase property can only be set through scripts.

For web sites, the ConnectionTimeout can be set either at the global level or at the web site level. To change the ConnectionTimeout setting, go to the Properties dialog of an individual web site or Web Sites node and under the Web Site tab change the Connection Timeout value. Even for FTP sites, the ConnectionTimeout can be set either at the global level or at the web site level. To change the ConnectionTimeout setting, go to the Properties dialog of an individual FTP site or FTP Sites node and under the FTP Site tab change the Connection Timeout value:

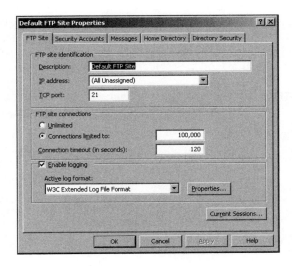

Configuring Compression Settings

IIS5 introduced the new feature called **HTTP Compression** that compresses the files before sending them across the network. HTTP compression provides a faster way to transfer connections from the server to the compression-enabled client using less bandwidth. This option could provide enormous performance improvement to the site. The following diagram illustrates the process of HTTP compression:

Figure 3

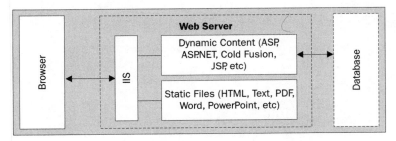

HTTP compression uses the industry standard GZIP (http://www.gzip.org) and Deflate algorithm to compress the data. Both the compression and de-compression algorithm is pre-built into Window 2000 OS and IE and above.

When a static file is requested from IIS 6.0 from an HTTP 1.1-enabled client, IIS sends the uncompressed file back to the client. Then IIS saves a compressed version of the static file in the temporary folder and, for subsequent requests, IIS will serve the compressed file back to the HTTP 1.1 client. When the static file is updated, IIS will also update the compressed version automatically.

When it comes to dynamic content, the script output is compressed each time and sent to the client and is not cached in the temporary folder. This can put quite a burden on the CPU and the throughput could be affected by it. So use caution when using this option and also monitor the CPU usage on the server to make sure it is not maxing out to 100%.

There are third-party Web Server Acceleration Solutions available to make the dynamic content compression work and make it more scalable. The following list includes a few solutions (I'll leave the rest to you to explore):

❑　PipeBoost – http://www.PipeBoost.Com

❑　HTTPZip – http://www.port80software.com/Products/httpzip/

❑　ASPAccelerator.NET – http://www.intersoft.co.uk/ASPAccelerator/

❑　XCompress 1400 – http://www.xcache.com (Hardware solution)

We can enable HTTP compression on the server side by navigating to Web Sites | Properties | Service tab, and enabling Compress static files or Compress application files. You can also specify the compressed files folder and limit the size of the compressed files folder.

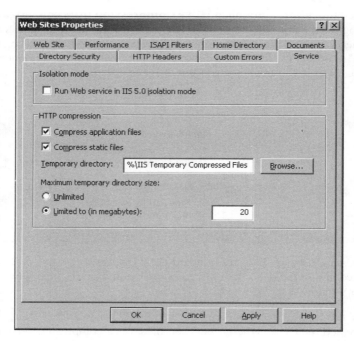

When you check the Compress static files option, only the HTM, HTML and TXT files will be treated as static files. However we can customize this setting using the HcFileExtensions metabase property of the <IIsCompressionScheme> node in the metabase XML file. In the same way, when you check the option or Compress application files only ASP, DLL and EXE file output is considered as dynamic content and this can be customized using the HcScriptFileExtensions metabase property.

HTTP compression will only work with HTTP 1.1 clients and can be enabled at the browser level. The following browsers support HTTP 1.1:

❑ Internet Explorer 4.0 and above

❑ Netscape 4.5 and above

❑ Opera 5.0 and above

❑ Mozilla 1.0 and above

You can enable HTTP 1.1 in IE browsers by navigating to Tools/Internet Options... and go to the Advanced tab. Scroll to the HTTP 1.1 settings in the Settings list box and check Use HTTP 1.1 check box. If you are behind a proxy server when connecting to the Internet, you can also select the Use HTTP 1.1 through proxy connections provided that your proxy server supports compressed HTTP content. Some proxy servers have a hard time coping with compressed HTTP content, so take some caution when enabling this option.

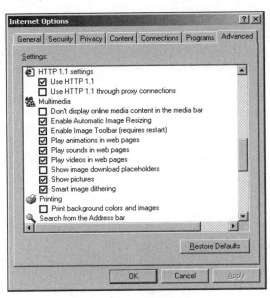

In Netscape 7.0 navigate to Edit| Preferences...| Advanced HTTP Networking and enable the Use HTTP 1.1 option in both Direct Connection Options and Proxy Connection Options sections (if you are behind a proxy server):

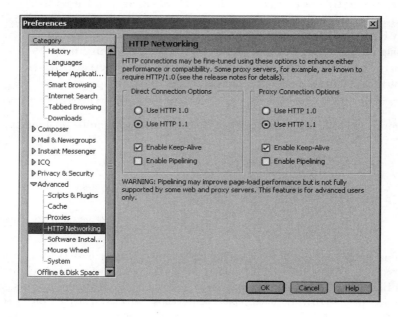

Summary

In this chapter we've take a brief tour of IIS 6.0 administration. We started the chapter with IIS MMC and then we jumped into command line administration. In command line administration, we learnt about the Net command and what is new in IIS 6.0. We've also learnt how to manage:

- ❏ Web Applications
- ❏ Web Sites
- ❏ Virtual Directories
- ❏ FTP Sites
- ❏ FTP Virtual Directories
- ❏ IIS Configuration
- ❏ Applications and Web Extensions

Then we learnt how to do programmatic administration using the WMI and ASDI providers. Then we moved onto remote administration and we saw pros and cons of different approaches includes IIS MMC, Telnet, WTS and web-based admin tools.

Finally we learnt what Quality of Services is and how to configure limiting connections, bandwidth throttling, application pool length, Keep-Alive, connection timeout and compression settings.

IIS 6

Programming

Handbook

6

6

Logging

For an administrator, collecting information about the activity on the web server is essential, and logging provides the ability to have your server keep track of all client activity. Information such as who visited your site, which pages were requested, and the results of those requests allow you to monitor site activity, determine the popularity of different content, and even diagnose problems such as bottlenecks and attempted security violations.

In IIS 5, all logging was done by the inetinfo process through COM objects. As there was only one inetinfo process, all web sites could write to their respective logs, without the fear of conflicts from other sites. With the new process model of IIS 6.0, web applications can be spread across multiple worker processes and application pools, thereby making it difficult to ensure that logging resources are always available. Problems can arise with multi-instancing and synchronization, when multiple processes need access to the same logging resource, as can be the case with a Web Garden, where multiple worker processes are active at the same time.

Thankfully, with the new architecture of IIS 6.0 these issues are not a concern, since most of the logging is handled solely from within the Kernel mode by HTTP.sys. A side effect of that fact, and one of the driving reasons for having HTTP.sys handle logging, is that it allows cache hits (which are served from within the Kernel mode) to be properly logged. However, ODBC (database) logging is still handled by individual worker processes, as typically the database handles the synchronization issues by itself. Custom logging is also handled by individual worker processes rather than from within HTTP.sys, as HTTP.sys is designed not to run user code for performance and security reasons.

In this chapter, we'll look at the different types of logging and how to decide between them, explore how to configure each type, and finally, how to make use of the logs generated by the traffic to your site.

Types of Logging

IIS 6.0 provides logging in the following formats:

- ❑ W3C Extended
- ❑ NCSA
- ❑ IIS
- ❑ ODBC
- ❑ Custom
- ❑ Centralized Binary

We will examine each type, which fields are logged under each type, what information they contain, and finally we will discuss which log format is best for a particular application. First, let's look at how we can select which type of logging to use.

You can select the log format from the Web Site Properties pane of a web site, which can be accessed by starting the IIS Manager, right-clicking on the web site name and selecting Properties. From the Active log format drop-down list on the Web Site tab, you can select one of the three, text-based logging formats (W3c Extended, NCSA, and IIS), or the ODBC format:

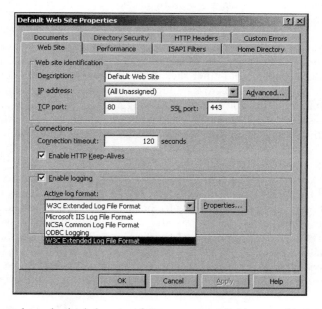

Once you have selected which logging format to use, clicking on the Properties button on the previous screen will bring up a Logging Properties pane:

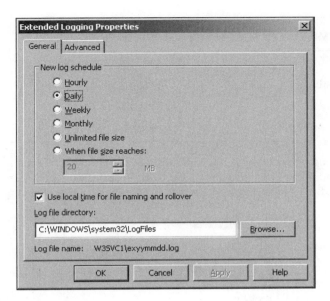

In the case of the text-based formats, this pane allows you to select how often to recycle your log files, as well as where to place them. Recycling your files allows you to ensure that they do not grow too large, as well as to facilitate easier use of those files. For example, selecting Daily will cause IIS to create a new log file each day, named after the date.

W3C Extended, NCSA, and IIS formats

These types of text logging formats are most commonly used, and are handled internally by HTTP.sys. This not only eliminates any issues with multi-instancing, but also ensures that cache hits are logged as well. All of these three types of logging provide the output in either **ASCII** or the local code page (**UTF-8**), if configured to do so.

W3C Extended

W3C Extended is a format standardized by the **World Wide Web Consortium** (hence **W3C**). Whereas the other two text logging methods (NCSA and IIS) that we will look at next are fixed-field formats, W3C Extended format allows you to select the fields that will be logged, with each field being separated by spaces. For the fields selected to be displayed, but for which there is no data, a hyphen ("-") is put in the place of that field.

Additionally, unlike other logging methods that use local (server) time, W3C logging uses **Coordinated Universal Time** (**UTC**, also known as **Greenwich Mean Time** or **GMT**) in its files. Log files of this type are named beginning with ex, followed by date sequence characters, and the file extension of .log. The date sequence characters represent the date of the log. The following table lists the filename formats for different options:

Frequency of Log Refresh	File Name Format
Hourly	`exyymmddhh.log`
Daily	`exyymmdd.log`
Weekly	`exyymmww.log`
Monthly	`exyymm.log`

You can select the specific fields that will be logged in the file. To do this, select W3C Extended option as described previously and click Properties button. Selecting the Advanced tab in the Extended Logging Properties pane brings up the following pane:

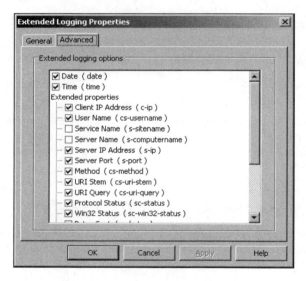

The various options that are provided by the W3C Extended format are as follows:

W3C Extended Logging Field	Description
Client IP Address	The IP address of the client accessing your site
User Name	The name of the client accessing your site
Service Name	The Internet service and instance number that was accessed by client
Server Name	The name of your server
Server IP	The IP address of your server

W3C Extended Logging Field	Description
Server Port	The port that the client accesses
Method	The action performed (GET, POST, and others)
URI Stem	The accessed resource
URI Query	The contents of the query string
Protocol Status	The HTTP status code returned
Win32 Status	The Windows status code returned
Bytes Sent	The number of bytes sent by your site
Bytes Received	The number of bytes received by your site
Time Taken	Time taken (in milliseconds) to service the request
Protocol Version	The protocol version used (for example, HTTP 1.1)
Host	The host computer name
User Agent	The client browser
Cookie	Any cookie sent or received
Referrer	The site that referred the client to your site
Protocol Substatus	The substatus code (see *Using HTTP Substatus Codes*, later in the chapter)

In addition to these entries there are following prefixes that appear before the field values:

Prefix	Meaning
s	Server actions
c	Client actions
cs	Client-to-server actions
sc	Server-to-client actions

A typical entry in a W3C Extended log file will look similar to the following example. The log file begins with comments including the software version, date, and which fields were selected.

```
#Software: Microsoft Internet Information Services 6.0
#Version: 1.0
#Date: 2003-02-07 09:00:02
```

```
#Fields: date time s-ip cs-method cs-uri-stem cs-uri-query s-port cs-
username c-ip cs(User-Agent) cs(Referer) sc-status sc-substatus sc-
win32-status

2003-02-07 09:00:02 192.168.2.2 GET
/pictures/Disneyland/Fireworks04.htm - 80 - 66.12.180.42
Mozilla/2.0+(compatible;+Ask+Jeeves/Teoma) - 200 0 0

2003-02-07 10:08:01 192.168.2.2 GET /rss.xml - 80 - 66.12.180.42
Syndic8/1.0+(http://www.syndic8.com/) - 200 0 0

2003-02-08 01:22:56 192.168.2.2 GET /Studio/Default.htm - 80 -
66.12.180.42
Mozilla/4.0+(compatible;+MSIE+6.0;+Windows+98;+Win+9x+4.90)
http://www.reasonstation.net/board/viewtopic.phtml 200 0 0
```

In these three entries, we see a successful page request from a search engine (in this case, Ask Jeeves), a request for the site's RSS file for blog syndication, and a request for the Default.htm page in the site's Studio directory. The last example is notable in that it contains an entry for the cs(Referrer) field, indicating that this request came as a result of a link elsewhere. This field is significantly useful in finding those sites from where hits on your web site are originating.

NCSA

NCSA (**National Center for Supercomputing Applications**) format is a fixed-field format. In other words, it contains a set number of fields, which cannot be modified. Items are separated by spaces, and the time is the local server time. Log files of this type are named beginning with nc.

This format is available for web, but not FTP, logging. The various fields that are logged are as follows:

NCSA Logging Field	Description
Remote Host Name	The name (or IP address) of the client accessing your site.
Remote Log Name	Remote user log name. IIS always places a dash ("-") in this field.
User Name	Name of the user accessing your site. An anonymous user will be represented by a dash.
Date	The date of the request.
Time and GMT Offset	The time and offset from GMT of the request.
Request/Version	The request served (including the query string) and the protocol version used (HTTP 1.1, for example).
Service Status Code	The HTTP status code returned.
Bytes Sent	The number of bytes sent by your site.

A typical entry in NCSA format might look like:

```
192.168.2.2 - chris [12/Feb/2003:10:22:42 -0800] "GET
/default.aspx?section=BurningMan HTTP/1.1" 200 8860
```

Each field corresponds to the appropriate field in the previous table; the first being the remote host, then the user name, followed by the date and time, and then the request (in this case, a request for the `default.aspx` page). The status code comes next, followed by the number of bytes sent.

IIS

IIS logging format is also a fixed-field format, though it has more available data than NCSA format. The IIS format includes basic information such as the client's IP address, date, time, as well as more detailed information such as time elapsed and the bytes sent. All items are separated by commas, and the time is the local server time. Log files of this type are named beginning with `in`.

The different fields provided by the IIS logging format are:

IIS Logging Field	Description
IP Address of User	The IP address of the client accessing your site
User Name	The name of the user accessing your site
Date	The date of the request
Time	The time of the request
Service and Instance	The service instance name (for example, W3SVC3)
Computer Name	The name of your server
IP Address of Server	The IP address of your server
Time Taken	Time taken (in milliseconds) to service the request
Bytes Sent	The number of bytes sent by your site
Bytes Received	The number of bytes received by your site
Service Status Code	The HTTP or FTP status code returned
Windows Status Code	The Windows status code returned
Request Type	The action performed (GET, POST, and others)
Target of the operation	The file served
Parameters	The query string contents

A typical entry in IIS format might look like:

```
192.168.2.4, -, 02/22/03, 19:42:32, W3SVC1, HOUSE, 66.12.65.12, 4209,
150, 8900, 200, 0, GET, /default.aspx,story=GoSLOPunks,
```

In this case, we see a request from a client at 192.168.2.4 for the machine HOUSE located at 66.12.65.12, on 22 February 2003 at 42 minutes after seven in the evening. The server took 4209 milliseconds to process a GET request for detault.aspx with a query string of story=GoSLOPunks. The request was a total of 150 bytes, and the server returned a 200 status code (indicating success) and 8900 bytes of data.

> **Entries in IIS format always end in a trailing comma, and then a carriage return and linefeed pair.**

You may realize at this point that both IIS and NCSA are subsets of the fields available in W3C Extended. Naturally, W3C Extended is the most commonly used text logging format by far.

ODBC Logging

ODBC logging is a fixed-field format that uses **Open Database Connectivity** calls to send the logging information to a database. As databases are typically capable of handling multiple simultaneous transactions, ODBC logging is handled within each worker process.

! **Requests that are served by the HTTP.sys URI cache will not be logged when using ODBC logging, as the requests do not reach the worker process.**

You can select the ODBC logging format in the Active log format drop-down box in the Web Site property page of the web site, as we have seen previously. By clicking on the Properties button next, you can set various parameters in the ODBC Logging Properties pane:

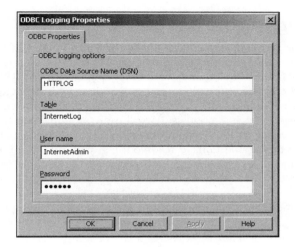

The different fields provided by ODBC logging format are:

ODBC Logging Field	Data Type	Description
ClientHost	varchar(255)	The name (or IP address) of the client accessing your site
Username	varchar(255)	The name of the user accessing your site
LogTime	datetime	The date and time of the request
Service	varchar(255)	The name of the service accessed
Machine	varchar(255)	The name of your server
ServerIP	varchar(50)	The IP address of your server
ProcessingTime	int	The amount of time taken to process the request
BytesRecvd	int	The number of bytes received by your site
BytesSent	int	The number of bytes sent by your site
ServiceStatus	int	The HTTP status code returned
Win32Status	int	The Windows status code returned
Operation	varchar(255)	The action performed (GET, POST, and others)
Target	varchar(255)	The file served
Parameters	varchar(255)	The query string contents

Custom Logging

Custom logging is accomplished by a COM object, which implements the `ILogPlugin` or `ILogPluginEx` interface written to handle IIS logging. Once registered, the COM objects that handle custom logging have their GUID placed in the `LogPluginClsid` metabase property to ensure that they are instantiated and used. While `ILogPlugin` is required, more interfaces will optionally provide enhanced functionality to custom logging modules. IIS will use your implementation of the `ILogUIPlugin` interface to allow administrators to perform any configuration on your module. To allow other applications to read your log, you can also implement the `ILogScripting` interface, allowing applications to use the `LogScripting` object to parse your log files.

In other logging methods, `HTTP.sys` uses the LocalSystem account for logging. When using custom logging, however, the logging module is run under the same account as the application pool for which it is active.

Since each worker process handles custom logging, there is a problem with synchronization in the case where multiple worker processes are attempting to log to the same source. However, a number of workaround actions can be implemented, such as:

❑ Ensure that all applications are running in a single application pool

❑ Ensure that there is only one process in the application pool. In other words, do not enable a Web Garden

❑ Disable overlapping recycling of worker processes to ensure that there is only one process active at any given time

! Requests that are served by the `HTTP.sys` URI cache will not be logged when using custom logging, as the requests do not reach the worker process.

Centralized Binary Logging

Centralized binary logging allows multiple web applications to write to a single unformatted binary log, reducing memory use, and providing a moderate increase in performance and scalability. This is due to reduction in the number of log file buffers needed, especially in cases where a server hosts a large number of web sites. With hundreds, or even thousands of web sites on a server, considerable memory and CPU usage can occur in creating a large number of logging buffers and formatting them to write to hundreds of individual log files.

Centralized Binary logging will cause all web sites to write to the single log file conserving resources, as only one log file is in use and is written in the binary form, eliminating the need to format the output. This type of logging is controlled at the server level, rather than the site level. In other words, you must have all sites use Centralized Binary logging if you choose to employ this logging method, disabling all other methods for all sites on your server. Log files of this type are named beginning with raw and have an extension of .ibl.

The **IIS 6.0 Resource Kit** ships with a log parsing tool, and the **IIS 6.0 Software Development Kit** (**SDK**) contains the header file and format information for binary logging.

UTF-8 Logging

IIS 6.0 now has the capability to write log files in UTF-8 if so selected. What this means is that log files may now contain the URL and query information passed to the server in the native language used, allowing more accurate tracking of actual usage.

! **UTF8 is for web logging only, and is not supported for FTP logging.**

Remote Logging

In IIS 6.0, it is possible to specify a network location (for example, \\server\location) as the target for log files. While this method is useful for creating a centralized location for log files, it should be noted that there is a performance degradation, along with a potential security opening involved with writing log files over a network connection.

Selecting the Right Format

If you are like the vast majority of administrators, you will most likely use text-based logging, and utilize a utility to parse those logs and prepare reports based on their content. If this is the case, the W3C Extended format is almost surely the best choice for you, as it allows you to select which fields to log, and contains fields that are not available in the NCSA or IIS format.

If you need to store your logging information in a database, your choices are either ODBC, or writing your own customized logging module. In this case, you will probably want to use ODBC, as writing a customized module is decidedly non-trivial.

Finally, if your server requires the highest performance, and especially if you host a large number of sites, you should seriously consider centralized binary logging.

Using the Logs

Keeping logs of web server usage and then not making use of them doesn't make much sense. Most administrators are keenly interested in what is logged, what information is available, what trends are evident, and what facts about their server and its usage can be determined from those logs.

Using HTTP Substatus Codes

As part of a renewed focus on security, Microsoft has made changes to the information presented to the client when an error occurs. In general, the details of error information have been decreased to present as little sensitive information to the client as possible. This eliminates the potential security risks involved with providing information about a malfunctioning server such as detailed errors that expose sensitive information, or simply informing a potential attacker that part of your server is not functioning correctly.

However, this presents a problem to an administrator attempting to track down and resolve a problem, as most debugging techniques rely on the detailed error messages that are now unavailable. The solution adopted is to log **substatus codes**, providing specific information in the log files for tracking down problems.

Consider the situation of an IIS administrator who installs a new version of the **.NET Framework**, not realizing that this represents a new ISAPI extension. As discussed in *Chapter 3*, ISAPI extensions are disabled by default and must be specifically enabled. In this case, the administrator will begin to receive **404 Not Found** errors for ASP.NET pages that resolved before the upgrade. With substatus logging, the administrator can examine the log and see that the HTTP status code for the error is, in fact 404.2, which indicates that the request was denied due to an unlocked ISAPI DLL.

Determining Security Problems

Log files are excellent resources for detecting security problems, such as unauthorized access attempts and attempts by attackers to compromise your server. Take for example, the following actual log entries (the IP addresses have been changed):

```
#Software: Microsoft Internet Information Services 6.0
#Version: 1.0
#Date: 2002-09-17 05:05:43
#Fields: date time s-ip cs-method cs-uri-stem cs-uri-query s-port cs-
username c-ip cs(User-Agent) cs(Referer) sc-status sc-substatus sc-
win32-status
2002-09-17 05:05:43 192.168.1.2 GET /scripts/root.exe /c+dir 80 -
192.168.4.2 - - 404 0 64
2002-09-17 05:05:43 192.168.1.2 GET /MSADC/root.exe /c+dir 80 -
192.168.4.2 - - 404 0 64
```

```
2002-09-17 05:05:43 192.168.1.2 GET /c/winnt/system32/cmd.exe /c+dir
80 - 192.168.4.2 - - 404 0 64
2002-09-17 05:05:43 192.168.1.2 GET
/scripts/..%5c../winnt/system32/cmd.exe /c+dir 80 - 192.168.4.2 - -
404 0 64
2002-09-17 05:05:44 192.168.1.2 GET
/_vti_bin/..%5c../..%5c../..%5c../winnt/system32/cmd.exe /c+dir 80 -
192.168.4.2 - - 404 0 64
2002-09-17 05:05:44 192.168.1.2 GET /scripts/winnt/system32/cmd.exe
/c+dir 80 - 192.168.4.2 - - 404 0 64
2002-09-17 05:05:45 192.168.1.2 GET
/scripts/..À¯../winnt/system32/cmd.exe /c+dir 80 - 192.168.4.2 - - 404
0 64
```

These entries in the log file indicate an unsuccessful attempt at hacking a server. They indicate attempts to access potentially harmful applications (like cmd.exe, the Windows command processor). Note that each entry shows that the HTTP response code returned was 404 File Not Found. From this log, we can determine that someone at 192.168.4.2 was trying to break into the server, and take the appropriate action.

Analyzing Usage and Trends

If you run a commerce site, you are probably very interested to know how your site is being used. By counting the number of hits to your site and tracking where users are going, you can get an idea of which parts of your site are more popular than others. Especially useful is the cs(Referer) field, which tells you the URL of the page that the user came from if they entered your site via a link on another site. To know who is linking to you is very powerful information, as that link might be a product review or a recommendation of which you weren't aware. Tracking referrers is also valuable if you are running a banner advertisement campaign, as the referrer field can show you the sites that are generating the most click-through traffic. There are many commercial log analyzer packages available that can gather and process your logs to present you with a complete analysis.

Detecting Site Problems

As we've seen, the HTTP response code is part of the logged information. This is especially useful in determining if there are any design or functional problems with your site. Checking your logs for instances of HTTP status code 404 File Not Found can help you determine if your site has broken links. Instances of HTTP status code 500 can alert you to a misconfiguration of your server.

Security of Log Files

Since log files can be kept in any directory, it is imperative that proper security procedures be observed to protect them. More specifically, appropriate NTFS file permissions for access control should be set on all logging directories to limit access to log files. This is a critical security task, as log files may contain sensitive information. Consider the case of secure information sent over an SSL connection. Even in such a case, the contents of the query string are placed in the log file in plain text.

Summary

In this chapter, we examined the types of logs that IIS 6.0 supports, such as text-based logs like IIS and NCSA, which are fixed-field subsets of W3C Extended. Other formats include ODBC for database logging, customized logging modules, and the new Centralized Binary Logging. IIS 6.0 supports some new features such as support for logging in UTF-8, and remote logging. We compared each type in the context of making a decision on which to use, and we talked about how to use the logs generated to get useful information. That includes using HTTP substatus codes to track down problems, analyzing attempts at security violations, analyzing site usage and trends, and the like. Finally, we considered the security aspects of the log files and the directories in which they are placed.

In the next chapter, we look into the mechanisms of ISAPI filters and extensions.

IIS 6

Programming

Handbook

7

7

ISAPI

ISAPI (Internet Services API) is a programming model, which the developer needs to interface with to enable the creation of complex web sites. Complex web site development consists of the creation of dynamic page content that can be rendered on a web browser. In a static web page environment, the web page is usually pre-assembled, sitting on a web server, and waiting for a browser request. In contrast, dynamic page creation, that is more flexible than its static counterpart, enables pages to be created at runtime.

An example of this would be a snapshot view of a particular set of stocks from the stock market. If queries are made from the browser for the current stock prices, the page delivered now might differ from the page delivered later because of the fluctuation in the market. Some type of intercessor has to access a database or other storage medium, extract the current stock prices, and assemble a web page to represent the state of the market. In other words, some type of software application on the server must carry out the necessary processing, and then assemble the web page. In general, this is the role of ISAPI extensions.

An ISAPI extension is a program running on the server side which can build dynamic page content.

ISAPI filters, on the other hand, are used for a variety of tasks and some of those tasks include gathering web information for statistical reporting purposes, encryption, and custom authentication processing. An ISAPI filter is a program running on the server side, as is the case for extensions. They provide a type of pre-screening of the client request before it is passed on to the extension. Thus filters intercept the request before it is forwarded to the extension.

This interception of requests allows the filter to examine the request and modify it before it reaches the extension. As an example, a filter might provide custom authentication services that deny web access to particular individuals on a revocation list. By examining the username of the client request, filters can either grant or deny access. The most fundamental architectural difference between filters and extensions is that extensions are request-based architecture, while filters are event-based architecture. This will be covered in more detail later in the chapter.

We will cover the following topics in this chapter:

- ❑   Former ISAPI Models
- ❑   New ISAPI Features in IIS 6.0
- ❑   ISAPI And Security
- ❑   Developing ISAPI Extensions and Filters
- ❑   Debugging ISAPI Extensions and Filters
- ❑   CGI and ISAPI
- ❑   Is ISAPI For You?
- ❑   Object-Oriented ISAPI

Former ISAPI Models

Prior to IIS 4.0, ISAPI DLLs would load into the IIS core process. As a result, there was an implicit performance advantage over the future out-of-process deployment options (Refer to *Chapter 2* for more details on out-of-process execution). This was because an ISAPI component loaded in the IIS workspace could outperform the ISAPI components that were loaded into an out-of-process surrogate, in communication with IIS. This is due to the latency associated with making calls across the process boundary.

Admittedly, calls to in-process ISAPI components are always faster than equivalent calls to out-of-process ISAPI components. However, with this performance advantage comes a downside. Running faulty ISAPI components in-process (within the IIS core process `inetinfo.exe`) could crash the server.

Since IIS could host more than one web site concurrently, one system level error within an ISAPI component such as accessing invalid memory could crash the server, thereby terminating all sessions on all hosted sites. The following figure details the workings of an in-process ISAPI extension:

Figure 1

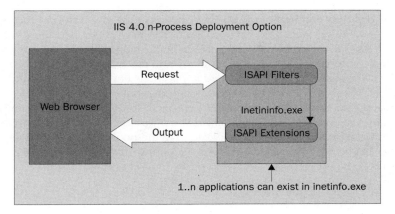

IIS 4.0

IIS 4.0 implemented a new deployment option known as **process isolation**. This allowed ISAPI extensions to run in a surrogate process space (dllhost.exe/mtx.exe), separate from the main IIS process (inetinfo.exe). This could be done while maintaining backward in-process compatibility with prior versions (as shown in the following figure). With the single out-of-process (single application per dllhost.exe/mtx.exe) capability, the server's susceptibility to crashes due to faulty ISAPI components was minimized. Of course, with improved fault tolerance came the concession to performance degradation. This is because of the need to facilitate inter-process communication between IIS and the surrogate process hosting the ISAPI component:

Figure 2

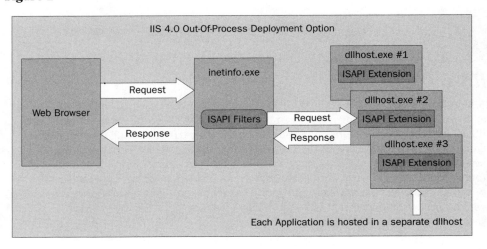

IIS 5.0

IIS 5.0 provided three application deployment options, two of which (in-process, out-of-process) existed in its predecessor, IIS 4.0. The new option was the **pooled out-of-process** option, which allowed multiple applications to reside in one pooled process, thus conserving system resources (shown in the following figure). The surrogate for hosting pooled out-of-process applications under IIS 5.0 also was dllhost.exe/mtx.exe. Since the application pool would run within dllhost.exe/mtx.exe, one system level error in an ISAPI component related to a particular application in the pool could crash the dllhost.exe/mtx.exe process. If an ISAPI component that served one application in the pool faulted, the whole pool would be jeopardized. Fortunately however, the pool would recover by being automatically restarted.

Figure 3

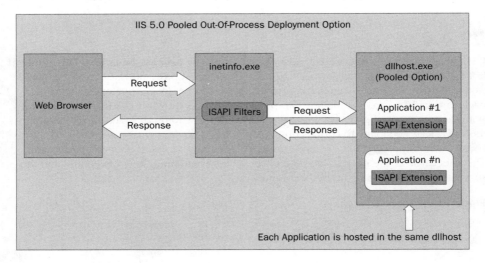

IIS 6.0

A key architectural move in IIS 6.0 is the separation between user mode processing code and kernel-level processing code. Even with an improved fault-tolerance scheme under IIS 5.0, the possibilities of injecting user code into inetinfo.exe still existed. Loading faulty ISAPI filters into inetinfo.exe could bring down the server, terminating all kernel-level client request processing. In IIS 6.0, the kernel level processing has been routed to HTTP.sys. Since third-party code is not resident in HTTP.sys, the kernel level processing cannot be encumbered by faulty user code, particularly developer errors within ISAPI components that would normally affect the health of the web server.

180

Furthermore, IIS 6.0 provides **kernel-level request queuing**. The advantage this offers is that IIS can continue to focus on servicing requests and not get involved in processing user code in ISAPI components. IIS 6.0 in a sense is the best of both worlds, that is, both the single application out-of-process and multi-application pooled processing models of IIS 5.0. The net effect is that the single out-of-process pool per server expands to multiple out-of-process pooled processing per server. So you get the benefit of having more than one worker process per server as in IIS 5.0, with each worker process capable of pooling. Not only does this pooled model conserve resources, but it also improves fault tolerance for potentially bug-ridden ISAPI components.

Application pooling can be configured as several worker processes per application pool. This is quite different from application pooling in IIS 5.0, in which the application pool was limited to one process. We know that the unit of process isolation in IIS 6.0 is coined "Worker Process" with a process name of w3wp.exe (WWW Worker Process). With the potential to have pooled processing in each worker process, resource conservation is achieved as in IIS 5.0. Another scalability feature in IIS 6.0 stems from the worker processes pulling requests from the kernel queue, thereby alleviating the kernel from having to forward requests as was the case in IIS 5.0.

A new paradigm in IIS 6.0 is the **Web Garden**, which achieves a high level of multiprocessor scalability. This is achieved by cloning a particular worker process up to n times. The upshot of this is that each worker process in the garden runs the same application or application pool (if the pooled option applies). The benefit of this architecture is that if a particular worker process is busy, other worker processes can share the workload. This load-balancing factor can improve throughput and overall efficiency.

Be careful not to confuse the Web Garden paradigm with that of Web Farms. Web Farms are the collective adjoining of web servers for load distribution. Web Garden is a paradigm defined in the space of a single web server.

In Web Gardens, it is a one-to-n relationship between one kernel and n worker processes. Also, each worker process or set of worker processes in the Web Garden can be assigned to a particular processor in a multi processor configuration.

The obvious benefit of Web Gardens to web performance in relation to ISAPI components is the parallel processing of such components. The HTTP.sys kernel-mode listener, load balances client requests by distributing workload based on matching the queue of incoming requests for an application pool against a queue of applications waiting for requests. This is not to say that Web Gardens and Web Farms are mutually exclusive architectures. On the contrary, we could have an IIS 6.0 Web Farm architecture, which implies n number of passive kernels, and then each passive kernel can associate to n number of worker processes. This architecture even increases the already heightened scalability obtained from Web Gardens. The following figure shows the workings of the worker process isolation option in IIS 6.0:

Figure 4

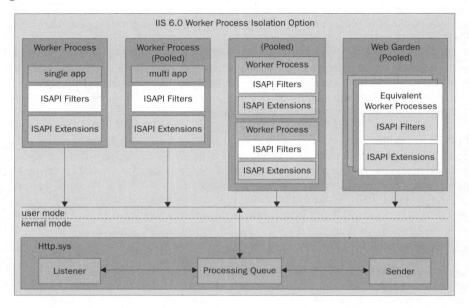

New ISAPI Features

IIS 6.0 introduces many new features for ISAPI that can be used by both developers and administrators. Significant changes have been made with the introduction of Unicode processing into IIS, the objective of which is to provide web client/server interoperability from multi-language participants.

Unicode ISAPI

IIS 6.0 provides new features for character sets requiring Unicode representation. The goal of Unicode is to have one character encoding to represent any character in any language. The problem is that the ASCII character set is not sufficient for all languages. Under the covers though, the problem is that an ASCII character is represented by a single byte. With a single byte the character set can include up to 256 characters. This is certainly inadequate character space to represent the plethora of characters in a multi-lingual world. Therefore, the goal of Unicode, to provide a universal encoding scheme for all characters, is accomplished with a two byte character which can contain up to 65,536 characters.

IIS 6.0 adds two new server support functions (callback functions that are utilized by both ISAPI filters and extensions) for ISAPI components to retrieve Unicode URLs. These support functions come in handy if your client sends you a URL request with Unicode encoding.

New ISAPI Extension Features

Additional functionality has been added to extensions that provide them with filter-like capability. The new features in ISAPI extensions are:

❑ Unicode Server Support Functions

❑ Unicode Server Side Variables

❑ `GetServerVariable()` Server Support Function

❑ ExecuteURL

❑ Global Interceptors/Wildcard Application Mappings

❑ `ServerSupportFunction()` parameter changes

❑ VectorSend

❑ RequestReportUnhealthy

❑ SendCustomError

Let's discuss each of them in more detail.

Unicode Server Support Functions

The following server support functions have been added for URL Unicode support:

❑ `HSE_REQ_MAP_UNICODE_URL_TO_PATH`
The function enables your ISAPI extension to map a logical URL path to a physical path

❑ `HSE_REQ_MAP_UNICODE_URL_TO_PATH_EX`
The function accomplishes the same with the added benefit of enabling the access to attributes associated with the physical path, like access control or cache control flags

❑ `HSE_REQ_EXEC_UNICODE_URL`
The function enables a parent ISAPI extension to redirect a URL for processing to a child extension which will perform the processing

More on this under the section *ExecuteUrl* and the section *Global Interceptors/Wildcard Application Mappings*.

Unicode Server Side Variables

One of the new features in IIS 6.0 includes Unicode versions of server side variables. Server side variables are maintained by the web server and are accessible to ISAPI extensions. Based on the content of these variables, useful decisions can be made in the extension. Querying the server side variables can give information such as the URL, server port, and remote host address. To access a server side variable in Unicode format, we just need to prefix the server side variable with UNICODE_. For example, if the server side variable were PATH_INFO, the Unicode equivalent would be UNICODE_PATH_INFO. The following table provides a list of server side variables:

Server Side variable	Description
PATH_TRANSLATED	Translates the virtual path to an absolute path on the file system. For instance the virtual path /profiles/managers might translate to /web/application/profiles/managers.
QUERY_STRING	Stores information that is part of the HTTP request that follows the ? symbol. This information is generally provided as useful input parameters for script processing on the server side.
REMOTE_ADDR	The IP address of the remote host making the request.
REMOTE_HOST	The DNS name of the requesting host. If the server cannot obtain this information, it will set REMOTE_ADDR and leave this empty.
REMOTE_PORT	The port number where the HTTP request originated.
REQUEST_METHOD	The method used to make the HTTP request, usually GET or POST.
SERVER_NAME	The server's host name, DNS alias, or IP address as it would appear in self-referencing URLs.
SERVER_PORT	The port number where the HTTP request was sent.
SERVER_SOFTWARE	The name and version of the web server software answering the request.
URL	Gives the base portion of the URL.

GetServerVariable Server Support Function

To access the server side variables, we can use the GetServerVariable() callback function. Here's a sample code snippet that does this:

```
GetServerVariable Code Example:

#define MAX_LEN 125

WCHAR strUrl[MAX_LEN];
DWORD dwUrl = MAX_LEN * sizeof(WCHAR);

pECB->GetServerVariable( pECB->ConnID,
                         "UNICODE_QUERY_STRING",
                         strUrl,
                         &dwUrl );
```

Headers can now be accessed with the HEADER_ prefix. The pre-existing HTTP_ prefix is still supported for header access as well. The key difference is that if HTTP_THIS_HEADER is specified, the server searches for a header named THIS-HEADER. If HEADER_THIS_HEADER is specified, the server searches for a header named THIS_HEADER.

ExecuteURL

This support function is present in the previous versions of IIS as the HSE_REQ_EXECUTE_CHILD function. If called from within a given ISAPI extension, the ISAPI component can delegate the URL request to a subordinating child ISAPI extension for processing. ExecuteUrl can be used to set up a chained processing environment, where the recipient child extension passes the request on to another child extension and so on. One use of this call chaining would be to allow the parent ISAPI to pre-process requests before forwarding them to the child component.

In the lpvBuffer parameter of the ServerSupportFunction() (explained a bit later), we can pass a HSE_EXEC_URL_INFO structure provided by the parent ISAPI, which instructs IIS on how to invoke the child ISAPI. Some points of interest in the structure are the pszUrl element which is the child URL (URL after pre-processing) to be invoked and the pszMethod element which is the new HTTP method seen by the child URL for processing. If NULL, this signifies that the HTTP method seen by the child will be the same as the parent.

Headers and request entity body information can be altered through the pszChildHeaders (type LPSTR) and pEntity (type LPHSE_EXEC_URL_ENTITY_INFO) elements. To pass the parent's headers to the child ISAPI, just pass NULL for the pszChildHeaders parameter. If the pEntity parameter is NULL, the child ISAPI has access to the unread request entity body. The element of the HSE_EXEC_URL_ENTITY_INFO structure of interest is the lpbData (type LPVOID), which points to an entity body supplied to the child ISAPI. The cbAvailable element is just the total number of bytes pointed to by lpbData.

The important thing about ExecuteUrl is that it can replace almost all read raw data filters. A common situation that necessitates the creation of a read raw data filter would be to examine or change the request entity body before the target URL processes it. To date, the only way to manipulate the entity body (without the target URL) is through the use of read raw data events. However, it is a daunting, often impossible task. ExecuteUrl enables an ISAPI extension to access the entity body and then pass it to a child extension for URL processing. Thus, ExecuteUrl makes the challenging or often-impossible crossover task of read raw data filter possible within the ISAPI extension

ExecuteUrlStatus

This support function returns the status of a serviced URL request. This function works in tandem with the ExecuteUrl support function. The ExecuteUrlStatus function takes a HSE_EXEC_URL_STATUS structure that will contain the information retrieved from the call. To use this function, call the ServerSupportFunction() function with a second parameter of HSE_REQ_GET_EXEC_URL_STATUS. Pass a pointer to the HSE_EXEC_URL_STATUS structure as the third parameter. Some elements of particular interest in the structure are:

❑ uHttpStatusCode
Returns the status code of the previously executed URL request

❑ uHttpSubStatus
Returns the sub-status code of the previously executed URL request

❑ dwWin32Error
Returns a Win32 error

Global Interceptors/Wildcard Application Mappings

Currently, IIS 5.0 supports one extension that can intercept, change, redirect, or deny every incoming HTTP request for a specific URL space. This is accomplished through the use of a single wildcard script map (*). This overall behavior falls under the category of Wildcard Application Mappings. This concept has been extended a bit in IIS 6.0 to include more than one extension to intercept all client requests through the use of the single wildcard scriptmap(*) thus yielding the term Global Interceptors. Wildcard Application Mapping enables an ISAPI extension to mirror some of the behavioral characteristics of filters.

Replacing Read Raw Data Filters

ExecuteURL and Wildcard Application Mappings provides the capability of replacing read raw data filters through the use of ISAPI extensions. The use of a read raw data filter is to peek at or modify the request entity body before the target URL processes it. To date, the only way to access the entity body was through read raw data notifications. Writing an ISAPI filter to accomplish this task is daunting to say the least. Now on the other hand, ISAPI extensions provide a much easier route for manipulating the request entity body. This makes an ISAPI extension the perfect candidate for replacing read raw data filters. After the extension pre-processes the request entity body, the request can be forwarded to a child extension for normal URL processing through the use of ExecuteURL.

ServerSupportFunction

The `ServerSupportFunction()` is a callback function that is utilized in both ISAPI filters and extensions. The `ServerSupportFunction()` callback is located in the `EXTENSION_CONTROL_BLOCK` (for ISAPI Extensions) or `HTTP_FILTER_CONTEXT` (for ISAPI filters). The `ServerSupportFunction` can be used to perform a variety of tasks. The prototype for the `ServerSupportFunction()` as applicable to filters is:

```
BOOL WINAPI * ServerSupportFunction(PHTTP_FILTER_CONTEXT pfc,
                         enum SF_REQ_TYPE sfReq,
                         PVOID pData,
                         DWORD ul1,
                         DWORD ul2);
```

Here `pfc` points to the `HTTP_FILTER_CONTEXT` structure passed the `HttpFilterProc()` entry point function. `SF_REQ_TYPE` specifies the particular support function to execute. The `pData`, `ul1`, and `ul2` parameters are optional and the context of their usage is dependent upon the `SF_REQ_TYPE`. If a parameter is not applicable, you need to set it to `NULL`.

The prototype for the `ServerSupportFunction` as applicable to extensions is:

```
BOOL ServerSupportFunction(HCONN ConnID,
                   DWORD dwHSERRequest,
                   LPVOID lpvBuffer,
                   LPDWORD lpdwSize,
                   LPDWORD lpdwDataType);
```

Here the `ConnID` parameter specifies the connection identifier of the client where the response should be sent, and `dwHSERRequest` specifies the particular request to be executed. As is the case with filters `lpvBuffer`, `lpdwSize`, and `lpdwDataType` are optional and the context of their usage is dependent upon the `dwHSERRequest`. If a parameter is not applicable you must set it to `NULL`.

Server Support Function Parameter Changes

There have been a few changes in the parameters that the
`ServerSupportFunction()` takes. The following table shows this:

Parameter	Changed to
HSE_REQ_GET_EXECUTE_FLAGS	HSE_REQ_GET_EXEC_URL_STATUS
HSE_REQ_EXECUTE_CHILD	HSE_REQ_EXEC_URL
HSE_REQ_IS_IN_PROCESS	HSE_REQ_REPORT_UNHEALTHY
HSE_REQ_VECTOR_SEND	HSE_REQ_SEND_CUSTOM_ERROR

HSE_REQ_NORMALIZE_URL, a support function addition, performs URL normalization
for extensions. The aim of URL normalization is that it helps to get to a resource. It
does not matter if the resource is an ASP, CGI, or a static file. For instance, if a URL
request has illegal characters, normalization would need to be applied to strip off the
offending characters.

VectorSend

This support function is useful because it eliminates the response redundancy
associated with request data in more than one file or buffer. Normally, response data of
this magnitude would be written out with multiple calls to `WriteClient()` callback
functions, which would incur more overhead than necessary. VectorSend reduces
multiple sends by enabling vectors of buffers and file handles that contain response
data to be assembled, which is then sent on a per call basis.

To utilize the VectorSend function, you pass the `ServerSupportFunction()` a DWORD
containing HSE_REQ_VECTOR_SEND as well as a HSE_RESPONSE_VECTOR structure. It
is a container for elements such as `lpElementArray` of type
LPHSE_VECTOR_ELEMENT, which is a pointer to an array of HSE_VECTOR_ELEMENTs.

SendCustomError

This support function enables the extension to send a custom error message to the
client. To utilize this functionality, you pass the `ServerSupportFunction` function a
DWORD containing HSE_REQ_SEND_CUSTOM_ERROR along with a structure of type
HSE_CUSTOM_ERROR_INFO that contains the error information. Some particular
elements of interest are `pszStatus`, which is a string containing the status line that
represents the custom error, as well as `uHttpSubError`, which contains the sub error.
If you don't want to send a sub error then set this element to 0.

RequestReportUnhealthy

The purpose of this support function is to allow an ISAPI extension to report to its containing worker process that it has become unhealthy and is requesting to be restarted. The extension can use whatever criteria it feels is necessary to determine if its processing state has become unhealthy. After the worker process is notified, it responds by setting the ISAPI Unhealthy flag to true. If the health monitoring system is active when the World Wide Web Publishing Service pings the unstable worker process, the worker process will send a notification to W3SVC requesting that it be recycled.

It is important to realize that recycling can only occur if the health monitoring system is enabled for the worker process. To utilize this feature, call the `ServerSupportFunction()` function with a second parameter of `HSE_REQ_REPORT_UNHEALTHY`. The `psz_reason_unhealthy` parameter is an optional field and can include a reason for the condition. The reason is logged in the application event log. If the parameter is not needed, pass a `NULL` value. As far as a return value is concerned, the `HSE_REQ_REPORT_UNHEALTHY` function is defined to return true.

New ISAPI Filter Features

The new ISAPI filter features are:

❑ FilterEnableCache

❑ Filter Load/Unload order

❑ `AddResponseHeader` Changes

❑ HTTP Error 400 Requests

❑ ReadRawData Notifications

FilterEnableCache

This new metabase property `FilterEnableCache` can be set for each filter, which signifies a cache-friendly status to `HTTP.sys`. `HTTP.sys` is the kernel-mode driver for IIS, which amongst other things listens for client side requests. The implication of marking a filter as cache-friendly is that the filter does not redirect URLs `/default.htm` to `default-1.htm` or `default-2.htm`, which would invalidate the cache's usefulness in this regard. The default state for filters is that of "cache unfriendly" meaning they don't redirect.

Filter Load/ Unload Order

In IIS 5.0 Isolation mode, the global filters (common to all sites) are loaded when IIS starts. The site filters are loaded (automatically) when they are added. All filters are unloaded when web service stops. In worker process isolation mode, the global filters are loaded in every w3svc.exe process. Also, each filter is not loaded automatically when IIS starts, but only when the site (for which the filter works) gets its first request.

AddResponseHeader Changes

In IIS 5.0, the headers that were set with this function were not sent in certain 401 responses. In IIS 6.0, these headers are sent in all responses after they are set.

HTTP Error 400 Requests

The HTTP error 400 requests that are rejected by HTTP.sys will not trigger a filter. However, this is not true for ISAPI filters that register for ReadRawData notifications.

ReadRawData Notifications

These notifications are not allowed in worker process isolation mode. However, they are allowed in IIS 5 isolation mode for backward compatibility. IIS does not load filters registering for this notification, when in worker process isolation mode.

ISAPI and Security

Let's take a look at some of the extension-based security issues in the following sections.

ISAPI Extensions Disabled by Default

In IIS 6.0, ISAPI extensions are disabled ("locked down") by default, which is a change in security policy from previous versions of IIS. This provides a safety net against attackers who might have an interest in stealing information from the server or crashing the system through well-known security holes. Therefore, extensions must be administratively enabled to activate them.

Process Identity

ISAPI extensions are DLLs, and DLLs live in processes. Since processes have a security context, ISAPI extensions take on the security context of their containing process. A security context is the set of privileges or non-privileges associated with the context. It decides whether the process can access resources or not access them at all. Each process contains an associated security token, which dictates access rights. By default, the security context of an ISAPI extension is related to what type of process it is loaded into. For example, if the ISAPI extension were to load into inetinfo.exe, the process identity would be System. If the ISAPI extension loaded in a worker process such as dllHost.exe or W3WP.exe, the ISAPI extension incurs a security context of IWAM_machinename.

Because server operations should be secure, server-side processing should be within the bounds of a client's privileges. In other words, the server should only be allowed to operate within the scope of the requested client's security context on the server. With this factor in mind, we need to have the default security context of the container process overridden by the security context of the requesting client.

Some extension operations can involve worker-thread participation. In this case, the threads inherit the same identity and hence the privileges as those of the process in which they are contained. If the ISAPI extension accesses resources, it is up to the extension to pass the security context of the logged-on user to the working thread. This transfer of security context occurs by passing an impersonation token of the logged-in user retrieved by the containing process to the pertinent thread.

Obtaining the Impersonation Token

When IIS processes a request, the client's authority to access resources is verified. This is because some clients might not have the authority to access certain areas of the server. IIS can be administratively configured to support one of five authentication schemes. The five options include **Anonymous**, **Basic**, **Integrated Windows 2000 (NTLM) Authentication**, **Digest Authentication**, and **Client Certificates**. If Anonymous is selected, the security context will be set to IUSR_machinename. If Integrated Windows Authentication, Basic, Digest or Client Certificates has been selected the security context assumes that of the account the user has logged in with on his/her client machine.

Once the security context is determined, the ImpersonateLoggedOnUser() function is called by IIS so that the current I/O thread is running as the authenticated user. The ISAPI extension is then called with the established security context. The extension thread can then access resources that are within the privileges of the authenticated user.

If the extension performs pending-based processing, this would imply the use of worker-threads for processing, which would necessitate the passing of the security context to the worker process thread. To pass the security context to the worker-based thread, the extension has to know what its security context is so that it knows what to pass. Remember that the extension functions in the capacity of the established security context, but has no knowledge of what that context is.

To know its security context, the pending ISAPI extension calls the ServerSupportFunction() function and specifies HSE_REQ_GET_IMPERSONATION_TOKEN as the value for the dwHSERequest parameter. The worker-thread uses the handle obtained returned by this call to obtain an impersonation token. The handle is valid for the lifetime of the EXTENSION_CONTROL_BLOCK, which is a structure that stores information like the request and client info (we will discuss this in more detail in the next section). The lifetime of the EXTENSION_CONTROL_BLOCK differs depending on whether the extension processing is synchronous or asynchronous in nature. If the processing is synchronous, the EXTENSION_CONTROL_BLOCK is valid until the HttpExtensionProc function finishes execution. If the processing is asynchronous, the EXTENSION_CONTROL_BLOCK will persist until the extension calls the ServerSupportFunction() passing a value of HSE_REQ_DONE_WITH_SESSION for the dwHSERequest parameter.

When the thread needs to access secured resources, it can either call ImpersonateLoggedonUser() or SetThreadToken() function, passing the handle obtained from the prior call to ServerSupportFunction(), which requested the impersonation token. The RevertToSelf() function can be called to end client impersonation and return the thread to the default security context of the containing process. For extensions running in an isolated process, the default security context is IWAM_machinename. For extensions running in the inetinfo process the security context is System.

Verifying Component Permissions

At times an ISAPI extension could invoke a COM component, which fails not because the component cannot be created, but because the authenticated user does not have the privileges to create the component. To isolate whether or not the problem involves insufficient privileges, as opposed to just a generic object instantiation problem, you might consider the following: See if the COM component can be created from the server machine directly. If not, work to achieve this state. If it can be instantiated, you might check into the privileges that are necessary to create an instance of the component and make sure the authenticated user meets those requirements.

Developing ISAPI Extensions and Filters

ISAPI developers make use of ISAPI extensions or filters in their development efforts. Having a working knowledge of how to create ISAPI components is the focus of the following:

Developing Extensions

ISAPI extensions enable the creation of dynamic page content, taking web development to a more complex stratum than that of static page delivery. ISAPI extensions are request-based components, which means that a particular client summons the functionality these provide on a URL request basis. Look at the following URL and you will see what it means, http://www.wrox.com/test.dll. The DLL name would be the name of the ISAPI extension that processes the web request. ISAPI extensions expose three entry points or functions that are called by IIS. Also, IIS provides four functions that can be called by the extensions to perform activities like reading and writing to client. We will see these functions later in the chapter.

Extension Processing

Let's take a look at the inner workings of extensions. In general, extensions are summoned on a request basis from the requesting client. extensions can be programmed to fit within the scope of both synchronous and asynchronous processing which will be elaborated here.

ISAPI Extension Entry Points

As mentioned earlier, IIS uses three function calls that serve as entry/exit points for the extension. The three are as follows:

❑ `GetExtensionVersion()` : Initialization procedure

❑ `HttpExtensionProc()` : Extension code

❑ `TerminateExtension()` : Cleanup procedure

When IIS receives a request for extension processing such as http://www.wrox.com/test.dll, it first determines if `test.dll` is loaded. If not, IIS loads the DLL. After loading the extension, IIS acts as a broker or middleman between the requesting client and the DLL. IIS utilizes the virtual directory of the extension to map the extension into the URL namespace. Incidentally, you can configure your extension as a wildcard enabling all requests to that namespace to be routed to the referring extension for processing. (Please see the section titled *Global Interceptors/Wildcard Application Mappings* for more detail).

GetExtensionVersion()

After successfully loading the DLL, IIS calls the `GetExtensionVersion()` function in the loaded DLL. This function communicates registration information back to IIS. The `GetExtensionVersion()` function is passed a pointer to a `HSE_VERSION_INFO` data structure that gets populated with the extension's version information. When `GetExtensionVersion()` completes, it returns `true` indicating to IIS that the initialized extension is ready for use. However, if the extension returns `false` this indicates that something went wrong during initialization and the extension expresses its interest in not being callable by returning a value of `false`. The `GetExtensionVersion()` function is called only once when the DLL loads.

HttpExtensionProc()

Next, IIS performs minor pre-processing and then an `EXTENSION_CONTROL_BLOCK` structure is prepared, which contains the request data and pointers to callback functions (necessary for extension processing). After this data structure is prepared, IIS calls the `HttpExtensionProc` function passing it the `EXTENSION_CONTROL_BLOCK` structure. The `HttpExtensionProc` function is essentially the workspace where client requests are processed. The `EXTENSION_CONTROL_BLOCK` is a kind of multipurpose, bi-directional data structure, in that it provides the extension with useful input data for processing as well as output pointers to callbacks for calling into IIS.

Some of the data items in this data structure of particular interest are:

- ❏ `lpszMethod`
  Specifies whether a GET or POST operation is requested

- ❏ `lpszQueryString`
  Specifies the URL piece after the "?" mark

- ❏ `cbTotalBytes`
  Specifies the amount of bytes to be received from the client

- ❏ `cbAvailable`
  Specifies the number of bytes available at this point in time

If `cbAvailable` is equal to `cbTotalBytes`, then another member called `lpbData` will point to all the data that the client wanted to send. If not, then the member `lpbData` will point to data where the byte count consists of `cbAvailable` bytes. The data would therefore be less than the total amount of data intended to be sent by the client. In the latter case, the extension would need to use the callback function `ReadClient()` to read the residual data at the proper offset determined by `cbAvailable`. The function `ReadClient()` is stored in the `EXTENSION_CONTROL_BLOCK` structure as a callback or pointer to function. The range of return types from `HttpExtensionProc` includes what can be called "return before processing" and "return after processing" types.

❑ **Return After Processing**
Return after processing types would include those types that can be returned that reflect returning on a synchronous basis. In other words, IIS is blocking until extension processing is completed, and then control is relinquished from `HttpExtensionProc()` with the applicable return type (`HSE_STATUS_SUCCESS` or `HSE_STATUS_ERROR`). Subsequently, IIS can disconnect from the client and clean up any allocated resources. You can request that IIS keep the connection alive as an alternative. In this case, IIS would maintain state with the client, eliminating the need to recreate another connection for a subsequent request. The return type to signify this state would be `HSE_STATUS_SUCCESS_AND_KEEP_CONN`.

❑ **Return Before Processing**
Return before processing types would include those types that can be returned that reflect returning on an asynchronous basis. In other words, IIS is operating in a non-blocking fashion in the call to `HttpExtensionProc`. Then control is relinquished from `HttpExtensionProc()` with the applicable return type of `HSE_STATUS_PENDING`.

In a pending mode, the extension has queued the request for processing and will notify the server when it has finished. In this type of queuing capacity, a worker-thread could be created in the extension, where the workflow would take place while relinquishing control back to IIS. Once the business logic was completed, a notification would be sent to IIS to this effect. This notification is sent through the use of the `ServerSupportFunction()` with `HSE_REQ_DONE_WITH_SESSION` as a parameter. The `ServerSupportFunction` function is available as other callbacks in the `EXTENSION_CONTROL_BLOCK`.

Another return before processing type relating to asynchronous behavior would occur in the callback being positioned in the extension. This setup is in the form of a call to the `ServerSupportFunction()` function for transmitting a file to the client. In this case, IIS stores the transmit file request in an internal asynchronous I/O queue, while the extension returns a pending status code to IIS. Upon completion of the file transmission, IIS will call the extensions callback function.

TerminateExtension

After return after processing types processing, the `TerminateExtension()` function can be called when IIS decides it wants to unload the ISAPI DLL. As stated above, this function is optional and can be used to perform extension post-processing.

ISAPI Extension Callbacks

ISAPI extensions make outbound calls to the following functions:

- ❏ GetServerVariable()
  Obtains server variables containing information like the request and server

- ❏ ReadClient()
  Reads data supplied by the client

- ❏ WriteClient()
  Sends response back to the client

- ❏ ServerSupportFunction()
  Makes available a variety of functions that can be used by the extension to do its work

GetServerVariable()

The GetServerVariable() callback can convey information to the calling extension regarding the HTTP connection, the server itself, and CGI variables. The key parameters in this call are the lpszVariableName, which is the name of the variable for which information is sought and lpvBuffer, which is the recipient buffer which contains the requested information.

ReadClient()/WriteClient()/ServerSupportFunction()

As has been already mentioned, ReadClient() reads data from the body of the clients HTTP request. The WriteClient() function is opposite to ReadClient() and sends data to the requesting client. A good application of the read and write would be in posting a form to the server which would require ReadClient() to access form level data and WriteClient() to produce a response page.

Both ReadClient() and WriteClient() can function synchronously, meaning the extension is blocked until IIS finishes with either call. Both functions can operate on an asynchronous basis as well. To use asynchronous reading, you notify IIS of your intent to do so by calling the HSE_REQ_IO_COMPLETION support function through the ServerSupportFunction() function. You need to pass a pointer pfnIOCompletion to the callback function, which gets called back when the asynchronous read completes.

After proper callback setup, the next step is a request to IIS to begin the asynchronous read operation. This occurs by calling the HSE_REQ_ASYNC_READ_CLIENT support function as a parameter of ServerSupportFunction function. Next, the HttpExtensionProc function would return, indicating that the extension is waiting for a callback by returning a status code of HSE_STATUS_PENDING. When the read is completed or an error occurs, IIS will make a call to the callback function. The ISAPI extension can now process the newly acquired data and again request IIS to perform another read if more data is required. When all available data is read, the extension should inform IIS that it is done with the request by calling the ServerSupportFunction with the parameter HSE_REQ_DONE_WITH_SESSION.

There are two ways to implement asynchronous writes. The first utilizes an asynchronous `WriteClient()` function while the other uses the WIN32 `TransmitFile()` function, through the `HSE_REQ_TRANSMIT_FILE` function. In case you use the asynchronous `WriteClient` option, call the `HSE_REQ_IO_COMPLETION` support function through the `ServerSupportFunction()` to setup the asynchronous callback function. To start the write operation, notify IIS to commence the operation by calling `WriteClient()` passing the dwSync parameter `HSE_IO_ASYNC`.

If the `TransmitFile` option is chosen, set the pfnHseIO field of the `HSE_TF_INFO` structure to point at the asynchronous callback function. To start the write operation, call the `HSE_REQ_TRANSMIT_FILE` through the `ServerSupportFunction` function.

Terminate the `HttpExtensionProc` function by passing back a status code of `HSE_STATUS_PENDING`. Upon successful completion or error, IIS will call the callback function pointed to by pfnHseIO. The extension can again perform another write operation if more data is available to send. When all available data is written, the extension should inform IIS that it is done with the request by calling the `ServerSupportFunction` with the function `HSE_REQ_DONE_WITH_SESSION`.

Filters

A filter captures events triggered by a request. Thus, the relationship between a request and events is one-to-many. The same event can occur from two different requests and therefore the filter will be notified via the appropriate event. Again, extensions are concerned with processing a full request, while the filter is concerned about processing an event independent of the request that it's associated with. Filters offer a pre-processing capability in the sense that they have a crack at the request before the extension receives it. They also offer post-processing capability as it can access the response after the request is processed by the extension and the response is sent back to the client. In this sense, the filter is a bi-directional interceptor.

An ISAPI filter registers with IIS for particular events that it is interested in listening to. All filters that register to listen for a particular event will be notified of that event via handler code when it occurs. The sequence defined for filter notification order in the event that more than one filter registers for a common event is as follows:

Filters are notified according to their priority level in descending order. The range of priority levels is high, medium, and low. If two or more filters that have registered for the same event are also set to common priority level, the filter notification order is governed by the `FilterLoadOrder` property of the filter to resolve the order. Filters can be chained, so that all filters registered to listen for a particular event are notified. ISAPI filters can receive event notifications with each HTTP request that IIS receives, and each response that IIS sends in return. Filters can be viewed as global, because they are notified as a result of any request which presents a particular event for which those filters listen. There are two types of filters. The first is the site filter, which is a site-specific filter, and the global filter that supercedes all sites.

Fault Tolerance/Scalability Issues

Since requests funnel through the filters first, they can really tie up the IIS thread pool; a sure source for bottlenecks and reduced scalability. Of course, global filters minimize scalability beyond that of site filters because they are more encompassing and perform request processing for all sites.

In the IIS 6.0 Isolation mode, fault tolerance and scalability issues relative to filters still exist, but are more relaxed because the filters load into worker process as opposed to the centralized IIS kernel. One process where all filters exist is much more impeding than several processes that they are distributed into. Of course, with the new Web Gardens feature in IIS 6.0, scalability can improve across the board for filters and extensions, because of the cloning of worker processes and load balancing. Make sure that your filters are as fail-proof as possible before committing them to production.

Filter Processing

Let us explore the inner mechanisms of filters. Filters are event-driven as opposed to extensions, which are request-driven in nature. The relationship between the request and events is that the servicing of a request implies a series of filter events forming a one-to-many relationship. Filters provide bi-directional pre-processing of client requests to the server and server responses to the client. Filters operate on a synchronous basis, as opposed to extensions which provide synchronous and asynchronous processing.

ISAPI Filter Entry Points

Filter processing can be broken down into three areas: initialization of the filter, event handling, and termination. Each of the three is implemented as a function that every filter must support. Similar to extensions, each filter must contain the following functions:

- ❑ GetFilterVersion()
- ❑ HttpFilterProc()
- ❑ TerminateFilter () (this is optional)

GetFilterVersion()

To initialize a filter, IIS creates a HTTP_FILTER_VERSION structure and calls the GetFilterVersion() function in the containing filter, passing a pointer to the newly created structure. It is in this function that the filter expresses its interest in particular event notifications. This detail as well as a general priority level for the filter, version information, and other variables are loaded into the structure and passed back to IIS. The following table provides an ordered list of filter events. The ordering is a standard ordering but there are no guarantees on the exact sequence of events. Also, ISAPI code should not be developed that relies on a particular order.

Event	Description
SF_NOTIFY_READ_RAW_DATA	This event can occur multiple times per client request. The reading cycle occurs until all HTTP headers have been sent related to the request.
SF_NOTIFY_PREPROC_HEADERS	This event occurs once per client request. This event signifies server pre-processing of all headers related to the request, but not the actual data within the headers.
SF_NOTIFY_URL_MAP	This event occurs when the server is converting a URL into a physical path. This event notification can occur several times per client request. It will occur at least once after the SF_NOTIFY_PREPROC_HEADERS event. Additionally, it may occur several times throughout the processing of the request.
SF_NOTIFY_AUTHENTICATION	This event occurs prior to IIS authentication of the client. This event occurs as a result of establishing a connection or any time the user sends an authorization header with user credentials for authentication by the server.
SF_NOTIFY_AUTH_COMPLETE	This event enables changing the headers, version, URL or method sent from the client. This event is similar to the SF_NOTIFY_PREPROC_HEADERS but differs in that this event occurs after the client's identity has been negotiated.
SF_NOTIFY_READ_RAW_DATA	At this point actual script processing can occur. Script processing can occur in an ISAPI extension, CGI application, ASP script, PERL script, etc.
SF_NOTIFY_SEND_RESPONSE	This event occurs after request processing is complete but before sending headers back to the client.
SF_NOTIFY_SEND_RAW_DATA	This event can occur more than once and is the result of the script processor (ISAPI extension, CGI, etc) passing back data to the client.
SF_NOTIFY_END_OF_REQUEST	This event occurs at the end of each request.
SF_NOTIFY_LOG	This event occurs after the request has completed but before IIS logs the request.
SF_NOTIFY_END_OF_NET_SESSION	This event occurs when the connection between the client and server is closed.

HttpFilterProc()

Each time an event that a filter has registered for occurs, the HttpFilterProc()
function is called. As mentioned previously, filters can be chained so that all filters
registered to listen for a particular message are notified. As mentioned in the
GetFilterVersion() call, a priority level of high, medium, or low can be assigned
to the filter. The filters are notified according to priority level in descending order. If
two filters have the same priority level the call order is resolved by IIS with the
FilterLoadOrder property.

The filter becomes aware of the event type by examining the notificationType
parameter of the HttpFilterProc() function. After determining the context of the
call, the filter can perform custom processing using the pvNotification parameter,
which points to a notification specific structure, and the pfc parameter, which points
to the HTTP_FILTER_CONTEXT structure. Although events do occur in a recognizable
standard pattern, it is important to note that there is no guarantee on the ordering, and
your filters should not be dependent on a particular ordering of events.

TerminateFilter()

When the web service is stopped or unloaded, IIS calls the TerminateFilter()
function on all ISAPI filters that have implemented it. TerminateFilter() is used to
perform cleanup duties such as resource de-allocation. TerminateFilter() is an
optional function.

ISAPI Filter Callbacks

The callback functions provide a way for filters to communicate back to the IIS. What
is interesting about the callback functions relative to filters is that they are partitioned
into three different structures; two of which contain identical callbacks, and are passed
to the HttpFilterProc() function. This is unlike the ISAPI Extension, which houses
all callbacks in the single EXTENSION_CONTROL_BLOCK.

Callback Functions

The three structures that contain the callback functions are:

❑   HTTP_FILTER_CONTEXT contains following callback functions:

   • WriteClient()

   • GetServerVariable()

   • AllocMem()

   • AddResponseHeaders()

   • ServerSupportFunction()

❑ HTTP_FILTER_PREPROC_HEADERS contains the following callback functions:

- GetHeader()
- SetHeader()
- AddHeader()

❑ HTTP_FILTER_SEND_RESPONSE contains the following callback functions:

- GetHeader()
- SetHeader()
- AddHeader()

We will examine the callbacks in the HTTP_FILTER_CONTEXT structure first. The WriteClient simply sends data to the client. It takes a pointer to a buffer, which contains the data to send and the size of the buffer to send. The GetServerVariable callback can retrieve any one of several server variables. The lpszVariableName is a pointer to the string that contains the variable to retrieve. lpvBuffer points to the buffer that receives the value. For example, the REMOTE_ADDR server variable would return the IP address of the remote host that is making the request.

The AllocMem() callback function allocates memory on the process heap. The benefit of AllocMem() is that IIS will perform cleanup on this memory automatically when the session ends. In other words, you have an implicit garbage collector. The AddResponseHeaders callback allows the filter to tag on a response header for IIS to deliver to the client. The key to this callback is that it should be used before the HTTP_FILTER_SEND_RESPONSE notification, and not during or after this notification.

The ServerSupportFunction() callback can perform a variety of tasks, as is the case for extensions. The prototype of the ServerSupportFunction() is similar to that of extension in that the second parameter sfReq contains the support function to be called. One such support function SF_REQ_GET_PROPERTY can be used to retrieve IIS properties. For example, the fourth parameter, SF_PROPERTY_INSTANCE_NUM_ID, would retrieve the server instance for the current request.

One practical use of the server instance lies in the manipulation of the IIS metabase. The IIS metabase is a repository for storing IIS configuration information. To manipulate such storage, a handle to the metabase is required. To acquire the handle, it would be necessary to first supply key information, which could contain, in part, the server instance ID. Your architecture might have multiple IIS servers servicing requests, each having a particular instance ID. Knowing the instance would prove vital in acquiring the proper handle.

We will now look at the remaining two structures and the callbacks within them. One such callback `GetHeader()` simply returns the specified header. It takes a parameter `lpszName`, a pointer to the name of the header to retrieve and `lpvBuffer`, which receives the value of the header. The complement of `GetHeader()` is the `SetHeader` callback. `SetHeader` simply sets the value of a user-specified header. The parameter `lpszName` points to the name of the header to set while `lspzValue` specifies the value to set the header to. The two structures that contain these callbacks get passed to `HttpFilterProc` as the result of two different notifications.

Note that these callbacks come in two different structures which are discussed below:

❑ The first, `SF_NOTIFY_PREPROC_HEADERS`, notification occurs on a request basis. It indicates that the server has concluded pre-processing of the request headers, but has not commenced processing of the information contained within them.

❑ The second notification, `SF_NOTIFY_SEND_RESPONSE`, occurs after processing the request but before sending the headers back to the client.

Debugging ISAPI Extensions and Filters

Debugging ISAPI components with the aid of a visual debugger can really save you time as opposed to more primitive techniques such as error logging/lookup strategies. Stepping through the code all in one visual plane aids the developer in discerning problem areas quicker than primitive error log lookup techniques for problem determination.

To set up your environment to debug ISAPI extension and filters please follow the steps below.

Steps for attaching to a Windows process through Microsoft Visual Studio:

❑ Start the iisadmin service

❑ From Visual Studio, select the Attach to Process command from the Start | Debug submenu of the Build menu

❑ Click the Show System Process check box

❑ Select the `inetinfo` process from the list and click OK

❑ Start the W3SVC service

If your debugger is not capable of attaching to a Windows process, then you can perform the following steps:

❑ Double click Administrative Tools in the Control Panel

❑ Double click Component Services

❑ Select Services in Component Services

❑ Select the IIS Admin service and click the Properties button. Click the Log On tab

❑ Select the Allow service to interact with desktop check box and click OK

❑ Repeat steps 2 and 3 for all processes that run under the IIS Admin process, for example, World Wide Web Publishing Service and FTP Publishing Service

❑ Use the Registry Editor to add a subkey named inetinfo.exe to the HKEY_LOCAL_MACHINE/Software/Microsoft/WindowsNT/CurrentVersion/Image File Execution Options key

❑ Add the following entry to this new key
Debugger = DebuggerExeName
(where DebuggerExeName is the full path to the debugger you are using)

Your debugger will be launched when the World Wide Publishing Service is started. After your debugger is launched, you will be able to set breakpoints in your ISAPI component. Unless the extension has been loaded into memory you can't set breakpoints. If you are debugging an extension, start Internet Explorer and request the ISAPI DLL. After the page loads, you should enable it to set breakpoints. Refresh the page to activate the breakpoint. If the ISAPI component cannot load at all because of a startup load failure, you will have to load the ISAPI component before starting the debugging session.

CGI and ISAPI

Before the dawn of ISAPI, Common Gateway Interface (CGI), the scripting dinosaur of server side processing, had already made it's footprint. CGI accomplishes the goal of dynamic page production, transcending as ISAPI, the limits of static page delivery. However, the drawback of CGI scripting is its associated performance overhead. Each time a CGI script is requested, a process is created which loads the script to service the request. Thus, CGI scripting is a process per request architecture.

Figure 5

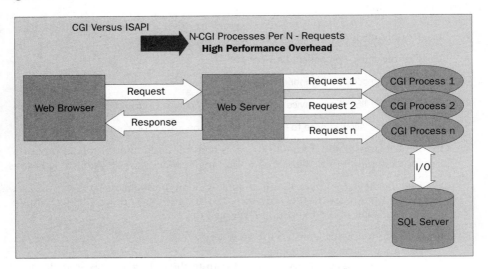

One can quickly see that if there were a number of client requests, server side performance would greatly diminish. Therefore, CGI scripting doesn't measure up to the expectations of processor scalability. ISAPI on the other hand is a much more viable option than CGI on a performance basis, as the ISAPI framework is not based on a process per request architecture. ISAPI Extensions can accomplish the same functional goal as CGI (see the following figure) with much less performance overhead (see section *Developing ISAPI Extensions and Filters* for more details). ISAPIs reside with DLL's, and therefore load into a given process space. As previously mentioned, the ISAPI paradigm does not exhibit the frequent request loading/unloading cycle evident in CGI scripting. ISAPI extensions once loaded, listen carefully for inbound requests to service.

Figure 6

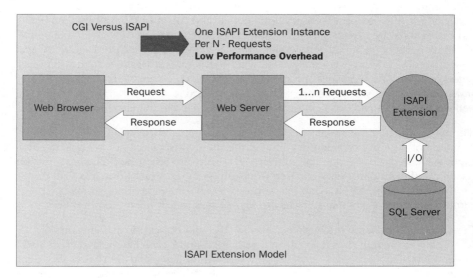

Is ISAPI For You?

Two useful perspectives to evaluate ISAPI's applicability or non-applicability in your development are maintainability and performance. From a maintenance viewpoint, ISAPI components can be code intensive because they are usually written in lower level languages such as C/C++. However, the price you pay in increased code intensity can be offset by increased performance due to the lower level manipulation. If performance is a high priority item for you, consider evaluating ISAPI on a time/delivery basis with other competing technologies such as ASP.NET, PERL, and so on. From the standpoint of platform independence, ISAPI is a specification and not a vendor-specific technology. Thus, ISAPI's applicability is not limited to Microsoft platforms.

Object Oriented ISAPI

In the process of developing your ISAPI applications, you might consider an object-oriented approach, unless of course you already have. Code modularity, reusability, and maintainability are some of the key benefits of an object-oriented approach.

The use of software modeling tools such as the Unified Modeling Language (UML) help facilitate an object-oriented approach to your ISAPI efforts; particularly if the ISAPI effort is part of a highly complex web development effort. UML is an efficient medium for expressing software design concepts. UML offers several design views which highlight specific aspects of an architecture. One particular view is the use-case diagram, which assists in really defining what the system will do. Defining what the system will do is generically part of the business process layer, which is the crucible of a successful project. The reason why ultimate software success and stability is tightly coupled to a well-defined and tuned business process level is realized in the effects of its absence.

Without a sufficient business process layer software malfunction is the effect. For instance not thinking sufficiently about all the different scenarios or actions, the system might leave gaps or holes in the software. The software might be behaving improperly because sufficient time was not given to charting out the exact flow. It is vital to map out the use cases in highly complex web projects because there are so many permutations of activity that it is easy to leave cases out or misrepresent others.

The connection between the business process layer and object orientation is one of developing a coherent class infrastructure with appropriate class inter-relationships to model the business process layer. This can be accomplished using the UML Class diagram. In the development of the class hierarchy, the goals of object-oriented design are realized.

Separating the business process logic from the ISAPI shell is another consideration. Often, it is tempting to write business process logic code within key entry points or event handlers. The drawback to this approach is that code reuse is minimized, as the code is tightly coupled to code areas that are not reusable. Separating the processing code from the entry points or handlers that encapsulate it will do wonders for reusability. If you can avoid the temptation to place your serious business logic code within the ISAPI entry points, such as `HttpExtensionProc`, it can be well worth it for current and future endeavors.

Figure 7

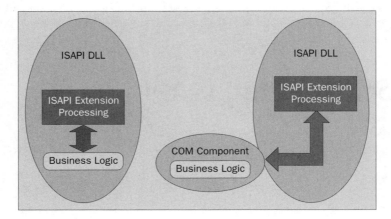

It might be better to package up your code (business logic or page creation code) in a COM component. Two main benefits of a COM approach are heterogeneous language interoperability and the location transparency. Heterogeneous language interoperability is the capacity for providers and consumers to communicate using dissimilar language bases, for instance, a VB client communicating with an ATL component. Location transparency implies using the functionality offered by a component regardless of where it is located. For instance, the component might be on the same machine as the client or on another machine on the network, which would not affect the working of the application in any manner.

Summary

In this chapter we have covered in detail the ISAPI Extensions and filters. We have brought forth much detail regarding the timeline of IIS deployment options and how they relate to ISAPI components in terms of configuration, scalability and fault tolerance. In the interest of multi-language support within IIS, we have covered the Unicode processing features added to the ISAPI programmatic model. In cognition of the drawbacks of filters we have seen how extensions can mimic filter behavior with the use of Global Interceptors and Wildcard Application Mappings. A detailed walk through has been given regarding security context and ISAPI extensions. Finally we attempted to encourage the use of Object-Oriented Programming practices with ISAPI for those who may be interested in it's usage. Here is a list of things that we covered:

- ❑ ISAPI Extensions adhere to a request-based architecture.

- ❑ ISAPI Filters adhere to an event-based architecture.

- ❑ ISAPI Filters provide a pre-processing zone for client-server request processing.

- ❑ ISAPI Extensions provide both synchronous and asynchronous programming models.

- ❑ ISAPI application development improves on the drawbacks of CGI based development.

- ❑ Worker process mode, Web Gardens and kernel level listening add rich architectural features to IIS which greatly improve scalability and fault tolerance for ISAPI applications.

- ❑ ISAPI Extensions and filters share some common three entry points. One for processing, one for initialization and one optional termination point. Both provide callback functions that are used to communicate with IIS.

IIS 6

Programming

Handbook

8

8

COM and COM+ Services

In this chapter, we will look at how IIS 6 differs from previous versions, in terms of support for COM and COM+ services. We will explore the new services and components that are available for programmers. We will also cover the .NET Framework and how it effectively integrates with IIS 6.

Threading

Let's start by looking into the new features provided by IIS 6 for ASP/ASP.NET developers in the area of COM threading. Before going into the details, let's have a look at threads and the various threading models available in COM and COM+. In a Windows application, a thread can be defined as a task or single path of code that is executed. For example, if we open an instance of Notepad in Windows, we are running a new process. If we type in some letters in the Notepad, a thread running in the background executes it. Similarly, if we print the information typed, it is executed by another thread, and so on. In simple words, any application running in Windows can be defined as a process whose actions are carried out by a number of threads working together in the background. These applications can be either single or multi-threaded with the threads executing them having various priorities for execution.

The five threading models available in COM are:

❑   Single Threaded Model

❑   STA (Single Threaded Apartment) Model

❑   Free Threaded Model (also known as Multi-Threaded Apartment model (MTA))

❑   Both

❑   Neutral

Single Threaded Model

A **Single Threaded** component has only one main thread for each application. The main thread alone is used to execute all the tasks related to the process. Since there is only one thread, it means that only one task can be performed at a given time and the application should wait until the task is completed, thereby deteriorating the system performance. To overcome this drawback, the apartment model was introduced.

Single Threaded Apartment Model

This model allows an application to have multiple apartments with a single thread residing in each apartment. Only one thread can operate in an apartment. If a thread from a different apartment needs to access data from the neighboring apartment, the data is to be marshaled between the threads to perform the required task. The execution of the threads is serialized by the COM message queue. This enables the users to perform multiple tasks at the same time without waiting for an existing task to be completed; thereby reducing the scalability constraints of a single threaded component, as discussed earlier. The following diagram shows different apartments and threads in single apartments:

Figure 1

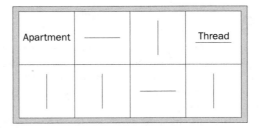

Free Threaded Model

A **Free Threaded** model is also known as a multi-threaded or **Multi-Threaded Apartment (MTA)** model. In this model, an application can have only one MTA in it. This MTA can have any number of threads within it. This model is a lot more advanced than the STA model. Whenever these threads need to share data, the data need not be marshaled via a proxy, as all of the threads are within the same apartment. Execution is a lot faster than STA. However the execution of the threads is not serialized by the COM message queue and it is the developer's responsibility to make sure that the thread execution is synchronized. The following diagram shows a multi-threaded apartment model:

Figure 2

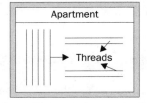

Both

There is another type of threading model called **Both**. This threading model is a combination of STA model and the Free Threaded (MTA) model. The advantage of this threading model is that no matter where the component is created, it will always be within the same apartment as the component that created it. If it is created by a component running in a single-thread apartment, then it will act like an apartment-threaded component, and be created in the apartment.

Likewise, if the new component is created by a component running in the multi-thread apartment, it will act like a free-threaded component and be created in the MTA. This will allow the components direct access to each other, since they are running in the same apartment. In either case, to access this new component, proxy calls are not necessary.

Apartment Neutral Model

The Apartment Neutral model is a new model introduced by COM+. This model overcomes the drawbacks in the free threaded model by taking care of the thread synchronization issues. COM+ allows any thread for a direct method call and makes sure that only a single thread accesses an object at any one time. In other words, this model performs the same job as the MTA model, without the developer having to bother about writing a thread safe code.

As we have seen, each threading model has its own advantages and disadvantages and it is left to the programmers to decide on the threading model that is best suited for the application developed by them. In the case of COM component, threading model for a component is determined at the compile time for each component.

The threading model used for a component can be determined by checking the ThreadingModel registry setting available under:

HKEY_LOCAL_MACHINE\SOFTWARE\Classes\CLSID\InProcServer32\ThreadingModel

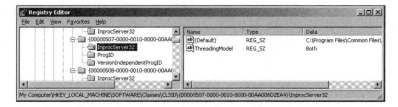

When the component is deployed in COM+, the threading model associated with the component can be determined by accessing the **Component Services** tool:

❑ Go to **Start | Control Panel | Administrative Tools | Component Services**, this will bring up the **Component Services** panel

❑ Here, select the **Component Services** node and expand it. Right click on the component deployed under the **COM+ Applications**, whose threading model needs to be determined, and click on the **Properties**. The **Component Properties** window appears.

❑ Navigate to the **Concurrency** tab

The threading model will be specified as shown below:

Let's now review the basic architecture of the previous versions of IIS with respect to invocation of components of various threading models from the ASP application, followed by the improvements provided by IIS6. In all the previous versions of IIS the scalability of the web applications greatly depended on the threading models of the COM components used by them and the scope at which the COM objects were defined. Also in the previous versions the ASP worker threads resided on their own Single Threaded Apartment. This created a problem when a free threaded/MTA component with application level scope is used in an ASP application, as the object has to wait until the main thread finishes execution.

Using IIS 6, it is now possible to run both ASP and ASP.NET applications simultaneously. The threading model of ASP.NET has been changed to MTA. But can the existing ASP applications running in IIS 6 run in MTA? The answer is yes!

In IIS 6.0, we can now modify the threading model for the execution of ASP applications and enable it to run in MTA. This can boost the performance and scalability of the application considerably, as discussed earlier. The ability to make the ASP application execute in the MTA mode is provided by one of the **metabase** settings available in IIS 6.

Let's find out how this can be done in the following section.

Apartment Model Selection

The ASP Application can be made to execute in MTA mode by modifying the ASPExecuteInMTA **metabase** setting provided by IIS 6. By default, the value of the setting is zero, since all the ASP applications execute in STA mode. To make the applications run in MTA, the value of the setting should be changed to 1 at the application level.

The administrators can manage and configure IIS 6 programmatically using the Windows Management Instrumentation (WMI) technology. WMI exposes a number of programmer interfaces through the IIS WMI provider object. WMI provider can be used to select and configure the IIS metabase. Let's now look at a sample ASP application, which uses the IIS WMI provider to change the ASPExecuteInMTA metabase property:

```
<%@ Language = "VbScript" %>
```

The following code creates the WMI provider object:

```
<%
Set mainObj = _
            GetObject("winmgmts://MyMachine//root/MicrosoftIISv2")
```

Create an instance of the IISWebVirtualDir object, to point to the root virtual directory of the first web site listed in the local machine:

```
Set VirtualDirectoryObj = _
            mainObj.get("IisWebVirtualDirSetting='W3SVC/1/ROOT'")
```

Set the ASP application to execute in MTA:

```
Response.write "Before Change " & virtualDirObj.AspExecuteInMTA
VirtualDirectoryObj.AspExecuteInMTA = 1
```

Save the changes to the metabase:

```
VirtualDirectoryObj.Put_()
```

Verify the saved changes.

```
Response.write "After Changing the Metabase Property" & _
               VirtualDirectoryObj.AspExecuteInMTA

%>
```

Before executing the ASP page make sure that the following conditions are satisfied:

❑   The Web Application Security should have the anonymous access disabled, because anonymous access is not allowed for any metabase property

❑   The Login user executing the ASP Page should be an Administrator

❑   The ASP process should have permissions to run the script

Save the above code with .asp extension and invoke it from the web browser.

One of the features, which was lacking in the old version of COM+, was the provision to install different versions of COM+ applications on the same computer and using them simultaneously. That meant a COM component configured/installed in a particular COM+ application could not be installed in a different COM+ application on the same computer. This drawback has been overcome by the introduction of COM+ Partitions, which allows multiple versions of COM+ applications to be installed and configured on the same machine.

COM+ Partitions

COM+ Partitions can be used to segregate web applications into their own COM+ applications (partitions). This is useful to prevent one web application from accessing the private COM+ applications, configuration information, and data of another web application. COM+ Partitions can help manage different versions of the custom COM components on the same computer.

For example, if you host web sites for two competing companies using COM+ in their web applications, you can use COM+ partitions to ensure that one company's web application cannot access the COM+ components in web applications of the other company. If one of those companies asks you to change certain features in a COM+ application that they both use, you can isolate the new version of that COM+ application in the partition that is linked to their web application:

214

Figure 3

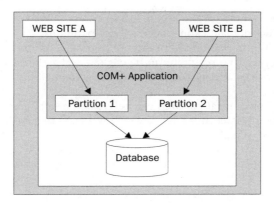

This facility is very cost-effective since it prevents having to use multiple servers for managing different versions of the applications. This is because on a single machine each partition can be made to act as a separate **virtual server**, with the applications contained in the partition. After the applications are installed in each of the partitions, the partitions can be further grouped into partition sets. These partition sets can be mapped to the users accessing the application contained in the partition. In the following section, we'll have a look at how the COM+ partitions can be effectively utilized by ASP developers in conjunction with the IIS 6.0.

A COM+ partition acts as a container holding different versions of the same set of components as different applications. Before the partition is activated, COM+ determines which component configuration to activate, based on the user's identity and access rights.

The **COM+ Server** (can be accessed by looking into Start | Control Panel | Administrative Tools | Component Services) has a system-defined partition, which comes by default after installation. This partition is known as the **Global Partition**. The Global Partition contains a standard set of COM+ applications and as the name suggests, all the users can readily access it. If you need to install an application, which is to be shared across all the users, it can be placed in the Global Partition.

In addition to the Global Partition, other types of partition can be created. These can be accessed locally in the particular server (**Local Machine**) and across the complete network domain. Creating these types of partitions other than the Global Partition, gives the applications the flexibility to control the users accessing it.

Local Partitions

Local Partitions are created for the access to local users of the computer. The users of other computers of the domain cannot access these partitions. The administrator of the machine can create a local partition and assign it as the default partition for one or more users of the server. The partition can be created and assigned to the users using the **Component Services** administration tool or programmatically.

Let's have a look at how a local partition can be created programmatically and assigned to the users using the COMAdminCatalog, which is a class that has the complete details about the COM+ Catalog.

The following VBScript code can be used to create a local partition:

```
Sub CreateLocalPartition(strPartitonGUID, strPartitionName)

    ' Instantiate COM+ Catalog
    Set objComcatalog = CreateObject("COMAdmin.COMAdminCatalog")
```

Access the partitions collection of the COM+ Catalog using the COMAdminCatalog object of the COM+ Admin Library:

```
    Set objPartitionsCols = objComcatalog.GetCollection("Partitions")
    objPartitionsCols.Populate
```

Get Reference to the Main Partition object to be added:

```
    Set objMainPartition = objPartitionsCols.Add
```

Assign the GUID and Name for the Partition to be created:

```
    objMainPartition.Value("ID") = strPartitonGUID
    objMainPartition.Value("Name") = strPartitionName
```

Save the changes and destroy the objects.

```
    objPartitionsCols.SaveChanges

    Set objMainPartition = Nothing
    Set objPartitionsCols = Nothing
    Set objComcatalog = Nothing

End Sub
```

The partition that is created will be available under Start | Control Panel | Administrative Tools | Component Services. Once the partition is created users can be assigned to the partitions. This can be done using **Component Services** administration tool or programmatically.

The following code demonstrates how to assign a partition to users:

```
Sub AssignPartitionToUser(strUserName, strPartitionGuid)

    Set objComcatalog = CreateObject("COMAdmin.COMAdminCatalog")
```

Access the Users collection and get the reference to the user object:

```
    Set objUsersCol = objComcatalog.GetCollection("PartitionUsers")
    objUsersCol.Populate
    Set objMainUser = objlUsersCol.Add
```

Specify the User Name and the GuID of the partition:

```
    objMainUser.Value("AccountName") = strUserName
    objMainUser.Value("DefaultPartitionID") = strPartitionGuid
```

Commit the changes and destroy the objects.

```
    objUsersCol.SaveChanges

    Set objMainUser  = Nothing
    Set objUsersCol = Nothing
    Set objComcatalog = Nothing

End Sub
```

Partition Sets

As we have seen earlier, partitions can be used to nest one or more COM+ applications within them. Similarly, a set of partitions can be grouped under the **Partition Sets**. Since the partition sets are created in the **Active Directory**, the users across the domain can access the COM+ applications contained in it. When the partition set is created, it is mapped to a specific user or group.

The user or group can thereby access multiple partitions and the COM+ applications contained in them, since all of them belong to a single partition set. Had there been no facility to create a partition set, each and every partition should have been associated with the users after creation, which would be a very tedious process. Thus the partition sets make it easy for the user or group of users to access multiple applications across multiple partitions, by having one-to-one association with the user of group.

When using local partitions, the default partition is assigned to users via the COM+ **Partition Users** folder in the Component Services administrative tool on the application server. When using partition sets in the Active Directory, the user's default partition is determined by the user's partition set.

Mapping Users / Groups to Partition Sets

As mentioned earlier, users and groups can be mapped to partition sets. By mapping groups to partition sets, an administrator can associate multiple users with a partition set at one time instead of having to map multiple user identities. A single user or group identity can be mapped to one partition set only. In general, mapping user or group identities to partition sets does the following:

❑   Ensures that applications are available to the appropriate users in the domain

❑   Helps COM+ in determining the partition in which an application is located

❑   Establishes a user's right to access a particular application

To associate partitions with partition sets within Active Directory and to map users and groups to those partition sets, administrators use the Active Directory Users and Computers, and Component Services administrative tools. When a partition is created within Active Directory, an administrator needs to locally configure that partition on the computer where the relevant COM+ application is to be installed. This local configuration of partitions created within Active Directory is done through the Component Services administrative tool.

Registering Components in Partitions

After a partition has been created, the next step is registering your COM+ components within that partition. A component is registered within a partition in two different scenarios:

❑   When a new COM+ application is created

❑   When an existing COM+ application is installed into the partition.

When the same set of components needs to be installed in multiple partitions, the partition service allows an administrator to copy the components from one partition into another. When a COM+ application or a component is copied, all associated partition properties are copied with it, except the users/groups mapped to the partitions.

Now that we have seen enough about partitions and how they work, let's move ahead and have a look at how IIS 6 can be configured to access the COM+ partitions.

Enabling COM+ Partitions in IIS 6

To enable COM+ partitions on the IIS side, set the `AspUsePartition` flag of the `AspAppServiceFlags` metabase property at the application level. The partition is identified by a GUID (created using the Component Services Manager snap-in), which can be set at the `AspPartitionID` metabase property. If no partition is specified, the default system partition is used.

The following example enables partitions on the default web site application (W3SVC/1/ROOT). It should be noted that after changing the `AspUsePartition` property, the `AspAppServiceFlags` changes automatically.

Instantiate the WMI provider object:

```
<%@ Language = "VbScript" %>
<%
    Set mainObj = GetObject("winmgmts:/root/MicrosoftIISv2")
    Set VirtualDirectoryObj =
    mainObj.get("IISWebVirtualDirSetting='W3SVC/1/ROOT'")
```

Set the partition flag value to 1:

```
    VirtualDirectoryObj.AspUsePartition = 1
```

Set the Partition ID to the GUID Configured in the Component Services Manager:

```
    VirtualDirectoryObj.AspPartitionID = "{00000000-0000-0000-0000-
                                          000000000000}"
```

Save the changes to the metabase:

```
    VirtualDirectoryObj.Put_()
    set VirtualDirectoryObj =    Nothing
```

Verify the changes:

```
    Set VirtualDirectoryObj = _
        mainObj.get("IISWebVirtualDirSetting='W3SVC/1/ROOT'")
    Response.write "After changing"
    Response.write "AspUsePartition=" &
                    VirtualDirectoryObj.AspUsePartition
    Response.write "AspPartitionID=" &
                    VirtualDirectoryObj.AspPartitionID
    Response.write "AspAppServiceFlags=" &
                    VirtualDirectoryObj.AspAppServiceFlags

%>
```

Tracker

COM+ Tracker is a new feature, which allows developers to debug ASP applications and know exactly where the error has occurred in the ASP page. For example, if a web application is causing problems on the server, the COM+ tracker can be enabled to determine when the ASP page is being loaded, when COM components are loaded, and when the components and page is unloaded. When the tracker is enabled in COM+ there is performance penalty. So after finishing debugging, the developer must make sure that the tracker is switched off, so that the application can return to its normal efficiency.

To enable COM+ tracker on the IIS side, the `AspEnableTracker` flag of the `AspAppServiceFlags` metabase property must be set at the application level.

The following example enables tracking on the default web site application (W3SVC/1/ROOT). It should be noted that after changing the `AspEnableTracker` flag, the `AspAppServiceFlags` changes automatically:

```
Set mainObj = GetObject("winmgmts:/root/MicrosoftIISv2")
Set VirtualDirectoryObj =
            mainObj.get("IISWebVirtualDirSetting='W3SVC/1/ROOT'")
```

Set the `AspEnableTracker` flag:

```
VirtualDirectoryObj.AspEnableTracker = 1
```

Save the changes to the metabase:

```
VirtualDirectoryObj.Put_()
set VirtualDirectoryObj = Nothing
```

Verify the changes to the metabase:

```
Set VirtualDirectoryObj = _
            mainObj.get("IIsWebVirtualDirSetting='W3SVC/1/ROOT'")
WScript.Echo "After changing"
WScript.Echo "AspEnableTracker=" &
            VirtualDirectoryObj.AspEnableTracker
WScript.Echo "AspAppServiceFlags=" &
            VirtualDirectoryObj.AspAppServiceFlags
```

Since we have already run the script through ASP, let's now run it through the command line.

❑ Save the file as enabletracker.vbs

❑ Open the command prompt and navigate to the directory in which the vbs file has been stored

❑ Enter the command CScript /nologo enabletracker.vbs

`Cscript.exe` is a command-line version of the Windows Script Host used for executing scripts. The `nologo` option has been used to display the changed values in the command prompt. The script will be executed displaying the values changed.

Fusion

Since the inception of Windows components, code and state sharing have been the primary areas of focus. In the early days, especially when people ran out of storage space, Microsoft focused on developing small sized components that were capable of being reused and shared by the existing Windows applications. Thus the **Dynamic Link Libraries** or DLLs were invented. DLLs are files that simply contain code, which can be shared between multiple applications and the operating system. As the Windows applications grew in complexity, each and every DLL was updated with new functionalities. When new Windows applications were installed in the machine, the existing DLLs were overridden by the new DLLs, which were supposed to have a superset of the existing functionalities.

More often than not, this gave rise to a scenario where an existing DLL has been overridden by the new DLL, which is not backward compatible. This resulted in crashing the existing applications, which used the old DLL. This gave rise to an interesting scenario, which got a famous name "DLL HELL". The word DLL HELL has been haunting windows programmers since then and Microsoft has been trying hard to overcome this drawback by introducing a series of technologies. These technologies have been grouped under the name **Fusion**. Let's quickly have a look at the evolution of fusion.

Introduction of Side-by-Side DLLs

The first solution proposed for the DLL Hell problem is the introduction of Side-by-Side DLL's, which was shipped with Windows Second Edition (Windows SE). This involved a concept where each application could use a renamed version of the existing DLL from the locally installed folders, thereby avoiding DLL conflicts.

For example, let's consider an application A (Windows 98 SE) that uses X DLL residing in Windows\system directory, and another application which uses a different version of the same DLL, installed in the same machine. Instead of overriding the existing DLL, the application can rename the system DLL and use it's own private version in one of the application folders. This prevents the possibility of incompatibilities and both the applications continue to run smoothly. This is a good solution, but the only problem is that it is manual and the developer must configure the applications for this feature to work. Moreover, this can work only with Windows 98 SE and not with the previous versions.

Windows File Protection

The second technology introduced by Microsoft for tackling the DLL Hell is the **Windows File Protection** (**WFP**), which was shipped with Windows 2000. This is a simple solution where the Windows system protects the overriding of the system-specific files by third-party applications. This too is a very effective solution, but with a few trade-offs which are worth mentioning. There may be a scenario where the new application needs an updated DLL in order to work properly. Since the WFP prevents the update of system DLLs, the application may not function correctly thereby crashing the existing system.

With the release of COM+ 1.0 along with Windows 2000, Microsoft made sure that the components installed in COM+ are not affected by DLL Hell. COM+ 1.0 allowed only one version of the application to be installed in the COM+ server. If a new version is to be installed, the older version had to be deleted. This made sure that the OS was not affected.

In the latest release of Windows Server 2003, Microsoft has overcome the sharing problem by effectively isolating the applications from Windows. This has been achieved by introducing the concept of side-by-side assemblies.

Side-by-Side Assemblies

Side-by-side (SxS) assemblies allow ASP applications to specify which version of a system DLL or classic COM component to use. This is achieved by maintaining the complete set of information about all the DLLs (assemblies) installed in the local machine. This information is stored in the form of an XML file, which is known as **manifest**. The manifest stores the complete information about the assembly and makes sure that the application never crashes, even if new versions of the assembly are installed.

Configuring SxS assemblies requires the following:

❑ The complete path to the DLL should be known

❑ The COM+ manifest file should exist in every virtual directory that is using the assembly (dll).

The IIS does not verify whether the manifest exists or not and it's the responsibility of the developers to make sure that the manifest file exists and is in the specified format. Otherwise IIS would return an error.

A sample manifest XML file is shown below:

Define the XML header information.

```
<?xml version="1.0" encoding="UTF-8" standalone="yes"?>
  <assembly xmlns="urn:schemas-microsoft-com:asm.v1"
          manifestVersion="1.0">
```

Specify the name of the assembly along with the type and version number.

```
<assemblyIdentity publicKeyToken="89948eh29="
                  type="win32"
                  name="New" version="1.0.0.0"
                  processorArchitecture="x86"/>

   <file name="Test.dll"
         hash="34hcdjkkjasdkksdflllsdff"
         hashalg="NEW1">
```

Specify the CLASSID, PROGID, threading model and the type lib information.

```
   <comClass clsid="{6D774676-0S87-49E0-A13D-DFH9753251}"
             progid=" Test.PathInfo"
             threadingModel="apartment"/>

   <typelib tlbid="{BBA55166-8BDA-516D-ZD12-1556666DD78F}"
            version="1.0"
            helpdir=""/>

   </file>
</assembly>
```

The side-by-side assemblies can be enabled in IIS both by using the IIS Manager and programmatically.

Enabling SxS Assemblies using IIS Manager

We can enable the SxS assemblies in the following manner:

❑ Right-click a web site or virtual directory and click Properties.

❑ Click the Virtual Directory tab, and click Configuration. If the configuration button is not enabled, it is because the application for this virtual directory has not been created. Click Create to create an application.

❑ In the Application Configuration dialog box, click the Options tab and select Enable Side-by-Side assemblies.

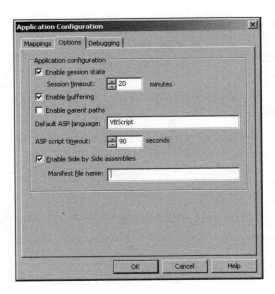

❑ Type the file name of the COM+ manifest file in the Manifest file name box and click OK twice.

To enable side-by-side assemblies programmatically, the AspEnableSxS flag of the AspAppServiceFlags metabase property should be set to 1 and the AspSysName metabase property should also be set at the application level.

The following example enables side-by-side assemblies on the Default Web Site application (W3SVC/1/ROOT):

```
Set mainObj = Server.GetObject("winmgmts:/root/MicrosoftIISv2")

Set VirtualDirectoryObj =
    mainObj.get("IISWebVirtualDirSetting='W3SVC/1/ROOT'")
```

Set the ASP application to enable COM+ side-by-side assemblies.

```
VirtualDirectoryObj.AspEnableSxS = 1
```

Set the AspSxsName property.

```
VirtualDirectoryObj.AspSxSName = "NewVersion"
```

Save the changes.

```
VirtualDirectoryObj.Put_()
```

The above code can be executed and verified either through ASP or through the command prompt as shown in the earlier examples.

Let's now move ahead and have a look at side-by-side assembly support provided by ASP.NET and how it is effectively integrated with IIS 6. The .NET Framework is supplied with Windows Server 2003 having all the necessary elements of ASP.NET included with IIS 6.0. ASP.NET is mainly an ISAPI filter that runs on top of IIS and processes pages with an .aspx extension. Using ASP.NET over standard ASP can significantly improve web applications.

The primary goal for side-by-side is to ensure that assemblies that are developed with different versions of the .NET Framework and common language runtime (CLR – Runtime provided by .NET Framework) can coexist side by side on the same computer. This applies to design, runtime and setup scenarios of the .NET Framework.

❑ **Design**
The .NET Framework provides design-time support, where different versions of Visual Studio can be installed and configured in the same machine, making the tools, compilers, and designers of each version act separately

❑ **Runtime**
The Framework provides the flexibility for the developers to install applications developed from different versions of .NET Framework/CLR in the same machine and makes sure each application uses its own version

❑ **Setup**
Multiple versions of .NET Framework/CLR and Visual Studio can be installed/uninstalled in the same machine without affecting each other.

Let's now see how the different versions of Visual Studio can be installed in the same machine and the tools provided by the .NET Framework to determine and configure the same.

Side-By-Side Support

. NET Framework exposes a component aspnet_isapi.dll, which can be used by the application to determine the version of the Framework used by it. The aspnet_isapi.dll is registered under the **IIS Script** mappings for each application virtual directory, and inherited by all the dependent applications in the hierarchy.

To configure the scriptmaps for an ASP.NET application to point at a particular aspnet_isapi.dll, the .NET Framework provides the aspnet_regiis.exe tool. The scriptmaps can be switched using the –s and –sn options of the tool. These options take the application root path as an argument.

A different `aspnet_regiis.exe` is shipped with each version of the Framework, and appropriate version of the tool should be run by the administrator/developer to register the application with a particular version of ASP.NET.

Windows Server 2003, ASP.NET and IIS 6.0

The latest version of ASP.NET ships in Windows Server 2003 (with RC2 release). The IIS 6.0 web server has introduced a new security lockdown console, which allows administrators to selectively enable/disable functionality in IIS. The registration process for ASP.NET provides a metabase key to be available as a configurable component in this lockdown console. This key is removed when ASP.NET is uninstalled.

During setup of the .NET Framework, there are provisions where the user can override the default setup settings. Instead of going for the express setup, an implicit installation can be performed using the `dotnetfx.exe` tool provided by the framework. The tool can be effectively used to prevent the automatic application upgrade during the ASP.NET Setup. For example the /noaspupgrade can be used to prevent the upgrade of the scriptmaps.

When a version of ASP.NET is uninstalled from a machine, setup will call `aspnet_regiis.exe` with the /u option (uninstall flag). Any application that is scriptmapped to the uninstalled version will be mapped to the next highest compatible version on the machine. If no compatible version exists, the scriptmap will be removed altogether.

The applications developed in different versions of ASP.NET should not share the same process between them during execution. Therefore the ASP.NET process model (`aspnet_wp.exe`) makes each version run automatically in a separate process at runtime. All applications that are developed targeting a particular version of ASP.NET share the same process (or processes under web garden mode).

In the IIS 6.0 process model (`w3wp.exe`), the process isolation for each application is configured manually. This has been achieved by the introduction of new IIS 6.0 feature called Application Pooling. In this feature, the applications available under the same pool are allowed to run together in one or more processes. However if the applications are assigned to different pools they cannot run under the same process (For detailed explanation on web gardens and application pools, refer to *Chapter 2, The new request architecture*).

Thus we have seen how the new features introduced in COM+, can be effectively utilized by IIS 6 and how ASP.NET has been well integrated to utilize the new features offered by IIS 6.

Summary

In this chapter, we've seen how IIS 6.0 provides support for COM and COM+ services. We started off by looking at the various threading models available and discussed the advantages and disadvantages of each of these. We also saw how administrators can manage and configure IIS 6.0 programmatically by using ASP applications and VB scripts.

We then looked at how COM can be useful to prevent one web application from accessing the private COM+ applications, configuration information, and data of another web application. COM+ Partitions can help manage different versions of the custom COM components on the same computer. We also saw a number of scripts to create and assign partitions to various users and also saw how to achieve this in IIS 6.0 programmatically.

We then discussed the newly introduced feature of COM + applications called the Tracker. Trackers are useful to debug COM + applications and know exactly where errors have occurred in an ASP page.

Finally, we saw how the DLL Hell problem was overcome by various techniques like Windows File Protection and Side-by-Side Assemblies. We saw how to enable side-by-side support in IIS 6.0 programmatically.

IIS 6

Programming

Handbook

Appendix A

Support, Errata, and Code Download

We always value hearing from our readers, and we want to know what you think about this book and series: what you liked, what you didn't like, and what you think we can do better next time. You can send us your comments, either by returning the reply card in the back of the book, or by e-mailing us at feedback@wrox.com. Please be sure to mention the book title in your message.

How to Download the Sample Code for the Book

When you log on to the Wrox site, http://www.wrox.com/, simply locate the title through our Search facility or by using one of the title lists. Click on Download Code on the book's detail page.

The files that are available for download from our site have been archived using WinZip. When you have saved the attachments to a folder on your hard-drive, you will need to extract the files using WinZip, or a compatible tool. Inside the Zip file will be a folder structure and an HTML file that explains the structure and gives you further information, including links to e-mail support, and suggested further reading.

Errata

We've made every effort to ensure that there are no errors in the text or in the code. However, no one is perfect and mistakes can occur. If you find an error in this book, like a spelling mistake or a faulty piece of code, we would be very grateful for feedback. By sending in errata, you may save another reader hours of frustration, and of course, you will be helping us to provide even higher quality information. Simply e-mail the information to support@wrox.com, your information will be checked and if correct, posted to the Errata page for that title.

To find errata, locate this book on the Wrox web site (http://www.wrox.com/books/1861008392.htm), and click on the Book Errata link on the book's detail page.

E-Mail Support

If you wish to query a problem in the book with an expert who knows the book in detail then e-mail support@wrox.com, with the title of the book, and the last four numbers of the ISBN in the subject field of the e-mail. A typical e-mail should include the following:

❑ The name, last four digits of the ISBN (8392 in the case of this book), and page number of the problem, in the Subject field

❑ Your name, contact information, and the problem, in the body of the message

We won't send you junk mail. We need the details to save your time and ours. When you send an e-mail message, it will go through the following chain of support:

❑ **Customer Support**

Your message is delivered to our customer support staff. They have files on most frequently asked questions and will answer anything general about the book or the web site immediately.

❑ **Editorial**

More in-depth queries are forwarded to the technical editor responsible for that book. They have experience with the programming language or particular product, and are able to answer detailed technical questions on the subject. Once an issue has been resolved, the editor can post the errata to the web site.

❑ **The Author**

Finally, in the unlikely event that the editor cannot answer your problem, they will forward the request to the author. We do try to protect the author from any distractions to their writing (or programming), but we are quite happy to forward specific requests to them. All Wrox authors help with the support on their books. They will e-mail the customer and the editor with their response, and again all readers should benefit.

The Wrox support process can only offer support for issues that are directly pertinent to the content of our published title. Support for questions that fall outside the scope of normal book support, is provided via our P2P community lists – http://p2p.wrox.com/forum.

p2p.wrox.com

For author and peer discussion, join the P2P mailing lists. Our unique system provides Programmer to Programmer™ contact on mailing lists, forums, and newsgroups, all in addition to our one-to-one e-mail support system. Be confident that the many Wrox authors and other industry experts who are present on our mailing lists are examining any queries posted. At http://p2p.wrox.com/, you will find a number of different lists that will help you, not only while you read this book, but also as you develop your own applications.

To subscribe to a mailing list follow these steps:

❑   Go to http://p2p.wrox.com/

❑   Choose the appropriate category from the left menu bar

❑   Click on the mailing list you wish to join

❑   Follow the instructions to subscribe and fill in your e-mail address and password

❑   Reply to the confirmation e-mail you receive

❑   Use the subscription manager to join more lists and set your mail preferences

IIS 6

Programming

Handbook

Index

Index

A Guide to the Index

The index is arranged hierarchically, in alphabetical order, with symbols preceding the letter A. Most second-level entries and many third-level entries also occur as first-level entries. This is to ensure that users will find the information they require however they choose to search for it.

X

WROX PRESS INC.

Wrox writes books for you. Any suggestions, or ideas about how you want information given in your ideal book will be studied by our team. Your comments are always valued at Wrox.

Free phone in USA 800-USE-WROX
Fax (312) 893 8001

UK Tel. (0121) 687 4100   Fax (0121) 687 4101

NB. If you post the bounce back card below in the UK, please send it to:
Wrox Press Ltd., Arden House, 1102 Warwick Road, Acocks Green, Birmingham. B27 6BH. UK.

Registration Code : 83929B8W2B3S8BR01

IIS 6 Programming Handbook - Registration Card

Name _____

Address _____

_____

City _____ State/Region _____

Country _____ Postcode/Zip _____

E-mail _____

Occupation _____

How did you hear about this book?

☐ Book review (name) _____

☐ Advertisement (name) _____

☐ Recommendation _____

☐ Catalog _____

☐ Other _____

Where did you buy this book?

☐ Bookstore (name) _____ City _____

☐ Computer Store (name) _____

☐ Mail Order _____

☐ Other _____

What influenced you in the purchase of this book?

☐ Cover Design
☐ Contents
☐ Other (please specify) _____

How did you rate the overall contents of this book?

☐ Excellent   ☐ Good
☐ Average   ☐ Poor

What did you find most useful about this book? _____

What did you find least useful about this book? _____

Please add any additional comments. _____

What other subjects will you buy a computer book on soon? _____

What is the best computer book you have used this year? _____

Note: This information will only be used to keep you updated about new Wrox Press titles and will not be used for any other purpose or passed to any other third party.

Check here if you DO NOT want to receive further support for this book.

8392

wrox

PROGRAMMER TO PROGRAMMER™